Ohio Government and Politics

SAGE was founded in 1965 by Sara Miller McCune to support the dissemination of usable knowledge by publishing innovative and high-quality research and teaching content. Today, we publish more than 750 journals, including those of more than 300 learned societies, more than 800 new books per year, and a growing range of library products including archives, data, case studies, reports, conference highlights, and video. SAGE remains majority-owned by our founder, and after Sara's lifetime will become owned by a charitable trust that secures our continued independence.

Los Angeles | London | Washington DC | New Delhi | Singapore | Boston

Ohio Government and Politics

Paul Sracic
Youngstown State University

William Binning
Youngstown State University

Los Angeles | London | New Delhi
Singapore | Washington DC | Boston

Los Angeles | London | New Delhi
Singapore | Washington DC | Boston

FOR INFORMATION:

CQ Press
An Imprint of SAGE Publications, Inc.
2455 Teller Road
Thousand Oaks, California 91320
E-mail: order@sagepub.com

SAGE Publications Ltd.
1 Oliver's Yard
55 City Road
London EC1Y 1SP
United Kingdom

SAGE Publications India Pvt. Ltd.
B 1/I 1 Mohan Cooperative Industrial Area
Mathura Road, New Delhi 110 044
India

SAGE Publications Asia-Pacific Pte. Ltd.
3 Church Street
#10-04 Samsung Hub
Singapore 049483

Acquisitions Editor: Sarah Calabi
Editorial Assistant: Raquel Christie
Production Editor: Olivia Weber-Stenis
Copy Editor: Erin Livingston
Typesetter: C&M Digitals (P) Ltd.
Proofreader: Jeff Bryant
Indexer: Marilyn Augst
Cover Designer: Candice Harman
Marketing Manager: Amy Whitaker

Printed in the United States of America

Cataloging-in-publication data is available from the Library of Congress.

ISBN 978-1-4522-9050-8

This book is printed on acid-free paper.

15 16 17 18 19 10 9 8 7 6 5 4 3 2 1

About the Authors

Paul Sracic chairs the department of politics and international relations at Youngstown State University in Ohio, where he also directs the Judge Sidney and Bert Rigelhaupt Pre-Law Center. He is the author of *San Antonio v. Rodriguez and the Pursuit of Equal Education* (University Press of Kansas, 2006) and coauthor of *The Encyclopedia of American Parties, Campaigns, and Elections* (Greenwood, 1998). Dr. Sracic's op-eds on American and Ohio politics have appeared in the *Washington Post, USA Today, Bloomberg View, CNN.com,* the *Atlantic.com,* and *The Diplomat.* Dr. Sracic is a former Fulbright Scholar in Japan, where he taught American politics at the University of Tokyo and Sophia University. He holds a PhD in political science from Rutgers University.

William Binning is the former chair and emeritus professor in the department of politics and international relations at Youngstown State University. He has a long history of being active in Ohio politics and government, holding both state and local government and party positions. In addition to coauthoring *The Encyclopedia of American Parties, Campaigns, and Elections* (Greenwood, 1998), he has written numerous articles on state and local parties and elections in Ohio. Most of these appear in biennial series: *The State of the Parties* (Rowman and Littlefield) and *The Roads to Congress* (Lexington Books). He has also published on minor parties with John Green in two editions of *Multiparty Politics in America* (Roman and Littlefield). Dr. Binning authored a chapter on third parties in *The 2008 Presidential Election* (Palgrave MacMillan). A slightly different version of that book was published in Italy. He occasionally writes on Ohio politics for the *Ripon Forum.* He holds a PhD in government from the University of Notre Dame.

Brief Contents

Detailed Contents

Tables, Figures, and Maps

Tables

Figures

Maps

Preface

This book is intended to meet the need for an up-to-date basic yet comprehensive text covering government and politics in the battleground state of Ohio. We want the reader to be able to grasp contemporary issues in Ohio politics but to do so with an eye on Ohio's political history and structures. As authors, we often debated how much data and how many details to include. We hope the reader will find that we struck an appropriate balance and that this book will be a resource not only for students enrolled in government classes at Ohio universities but also for Ohio citizens and journalists from around the nation (and world) who, along with the presidential hopefuls that they are covering, descend on Ohio every four years. As we argue in Chapter 1, Ohio serves as an apt microcosm of the United States. This is likely why Ohio voters have proved themselves so adept at selecting the eventual winner of our quadrennial presidential contests. This is also why a book on Ohio politics and government is necessary.

The unifying theme of this book is the idea of Ohio as a purple state. In a country increasingly divided into blue (Democratic) and red (Republican) states, Ohio remains among a handful of states that are not dominated by a single political party. Although Republicans have done very well in electing their members to positions in the state government in Ohio (most recently in 2014), Democrats were able to grab the state's electoral votes in both 2008 and 2012. Ohio has therefore become crucial to the strategies of both parties as they vie with one another for power. As American politics swing back and forth between Republican and Democratic dominance, Ohio's politics follow suit.

The book opens by explaining Ohio's role, now more than 50 years old, as the quintessential purple state in presidential politics. This is followed by a more in-depth look at the establishment of Ohio as a state and the evolution of the Ohio constitution. With this background in place, we move to a discussion of the various institutions of Ohio government. In addition to covering the legislature, the executive branch, and the courts, however, we include a chapter on regional and local government institutions. From this point forward in the book, we include in nearly every chapter a brief text box detailing a particular issue or event that helps to illustrate what was discussed. For example, in Chapter 5, when discussing the Ohio court system, we provide a detailed account of the court reform proposal recently proposed by the Ohio Chief Justice Maureen O'Connor. Other text boxes deal with subjects such as the debate over oil and natural gas hydraulic fracturing (fracking), political corruption and reform in Cuyahoga County, and the controversy over early in-person voting in Ohio. The text boxes are particularly useful in allowing us to draw the reader's attention to contemporary issues.

We then move to subjects that, although not altogether unique to Ohio, are fundamental to understanding the government and politics of the state. The first is the state budget. "Who gets what, where, when, and how" is perhaps the most famous definition of politics, and the budgeting process lies at the core of Ohio politics. Of course, like all states, Ohio has its own political culture, which was first introduced in Chapter 1. In Chapter 8, we circle back to this topic, looking at political parties in Ohio, the state's electoral rules, and the role of significant interest groups. Finally, we conclude by addressing the political procedures that Ohio shares with only a handful of states: the ability of citizens to participate directly in lawmaking via the initiative and referendum. There is symmetry to ending the book with this discussion. The initiative and referendum emerged from Ohio's early embrace of progressive political reforms in the early 20th century. At the same time, as the recent repeal of the law known as Senate Bill 5 (restricting public labor unions) shows, these reforms will continue to influence Ohio politics in the 21th century.

Although the faults of this book are solely the responsibility of the coauthors, we did benefit from the assistance of others. We want to offer special thanks to Henry Gomez, chief political reporter for the Northeast Ohio Media Group (and our former student!), who was very helpful to us as we sought to explain changes in Cuyahoga County government. Thomas A. Finnerty, project manager at the Center for Urban Studies at Youngstown State University, offered thoughtful comments on local government in Ohio. Jeffrey Dick, chair of Geological and Environmental Sciences at Youngstown State University, helped us to understand the issues surrounding fracking in Ohio.

CHAPTER 1

The Politics of a Purple State

"Operation Clark County"

A few weeks before the 2004 U.S. presidential election, Oliver Burkeman, a columnist for the British newspaper, *The Guardian,* came up with a rather audacious idea. Since he felt that the American election would have global ramifications, he urged his readers to take an active role in trying to influence the U.S. campaign. Specifically, he proposed "to match individual *Guardian* readers with individual voters in Clark County, in the crucial swing state of Ohio," so that the British citizens could draft personal letters to these American voters, letting them know how citizens from another country understood global political issues.[1] Not unexpectedly, the effort, branded "Operation Clark County," met with considerable backlash. Angry citizens from throughout the U.S. wrote hostile e-mails to the *Guardian,* accusing the newspaper of facilitating an improper and perhaps illegal attempt by non-U.S. citizens to change the outcome of an American election. The director of the board of elections in Clark County was even quoted as saying "the American Revolution was fought for a reason."[2]

In the end—at least from the point of view of the *Guardian* writer—Operation Clark County was a failure. Burkeman had hoped to convince voters to support the Democratic challenger, John Kerry; instead, Clark County was won by President George W. Bush, even though Bush had lost the county to Al Gore four years earlier. What is most interesting for students of Ohio politics, however, is to recognize that when it came time for a European newspaper to try to influence an American presidential election, the publication quite naturally focused on Ohio. Indeed, it would not be much of an exaggeration to claim that when it comes to U.S. presidential politics, the whole world directs its gaze to Ohio. Of course, they are just reflecting the behavior of the candidates themselves. For example, the *Washington Post* estimated that during their first term in office, either President Barack Obama or Vice President Joseph Biden visited Ohio on average once every three weeks![3] But is all of this attention justified?

Pittsburgh Post-Gazette

In the 82-year span between 1841 and 1923, the United States elected 21 individuals as president. Eight of those presidents, or nearly 40 percent, were from Ohio. Only the state of Virginia has sent an equal number to the White House (although, technically, the first president from Virginia, George Washington, did not occupy the famous address at 1400 Pennsylvania Avenue). Still, no Ohioan has sat behind the desk in the Oval Office since Blooming Grove native President Warren G. Harding's death on August 2, 1923.

Although no longer supplying presidential timber, Ohio has clearly remained at the center of presidential contests. The political mantra, repeated every four years, is that since 1960, no one has been elected president without capturing a plurality of the popular vote in Ohio. Unlike many such mantras, this one has the virtue of being true. As Table 1.1 shows, however, this does not mean that a candidate *must* win Ohio in order to capture the White House. Of the eight individuals elected in the 13 elections beginning in 1964, only George W. Bush (in both 2000 and 2004) needed Ohio's electoral votes to claim a victory. Every other president could have garnered an electoral majority without Ohio's votes. Moreover, in 2000 at least, President Bush, with only 271 electoral votes (one more than he needed) could not have lost *any* of the 30 states that he won and still claimed victory.

White House Historical Association

President Warren G. Harding

Table 1.1 does demonstrate a second important point. With every new census, Ohio's representation in Congress, and therefore the total number of electors representing the State, declines. In 1964, Lyndon Johnson gained 26 votes by capturing Ohio. When Barack Obama won Ohio in 2012, only 18 electoral votes were earned. In a sense, therefore—and again, by looking at the numbers—Ohio is becoming less and less significant in presidential politics. So why is Ohio still considered, even by the candidates themselves, a crucial battleground state in U.S. presidential elections? There are two related reasons.

TABLE 1.1 Comparison of Electoral Vote Difference to Electoral Votes Available in Ohio, 1964–2012

Year	*Electoral vote difference*	*Ohio Electoral votes*
1964	434	26
1968	110	26
1972	503	25
1976	57	25
1980	440	25
1984	512	23
1988	315	23
1992	202	21
1996	220	21
2000	5	21
2004	35	20
2008	192	20
2012	126	18

Data source: "270 to Win," accessed October 4, 2014, http://www.270towin.com/

When political pundits talk about *red states* and *blue states*, they are acknowledging that, even before anyone casts their vote in a presidential election, it is not hard to predict with a high degree of certainty which party's candidate will ultimately win the popular vote. Republicans dominate in red states and Democrats control blue states. So, for example, the two most populous states (and therefore the two most electorally rich states), Texas and California, are not currently considered competitive.[4] It is a foregone conclusion that Texas is red and will support the Republican candidate, while a majority of voters in blue California will cast their ballots for the Democratic Party's nominee. Texas and California are not alone when it comes to states that are considered noncompetitive. As Map 1.1 shows, a total of 38 states and the District of Columbia are considered fairly secure states for either the Democratic or the Republican nominee. That leaves 12 so-called swing states. Swing states are states where the outcome is difficult to predict because voters swing back and forth from election to election between the Republican and Democratic candidates. Swing states are also sometimes called *purple states*, since their electoral status is derived from the near-equal numbers of solid red and blue voters.

Map 1.1 Swing States

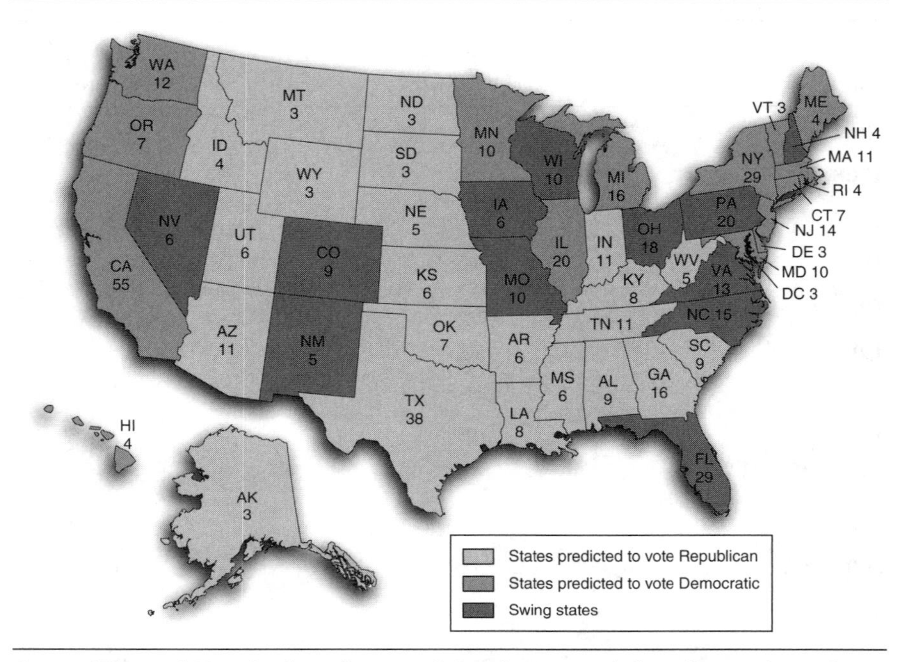

Source: "Electoral Vote Predictor," accessed October 8, 2014, http://www.electoral-vote.com/evp2012/Pres/Maps/Aug07.html

Using this definition, it is hard to imagine a state more purple than Ohio. For example, if one adds up all the Democratic votes for president between 2000 and 2012 and then compares that number to all the corresponding Republican votes during that same period, the difference is only about 150,000 votes out of more than 21 million cast. This comes out to a difference of less than 1 percent (see Table 1.2).

Looking at only the purple states in Map 1.1, one sees that only Florida and Pennsylvania have more electoral votes than Ohio. Since it is difficult to label Pennsylvania as a pure purple state (voters there having supported only Democratic candidates for president since 1988), among the truly purple states, Ohio trails only Florida in electoral clout.

Beyond electoral votes and the closeness of presidential races in Ohio, there is an additional argument to be made about the significance of Ohio in presidential campaigns. As Table 1.3 shows, Ohio is, demographically, somewhat of a microcosm of the United States. With the notable exception of the very low number of Hispanic voters in the state, Ohio looks like the United States. From this perspective, Ohio is important because it is an ideal test market for political candidates. Put

TABLE 1.2 Presidential Vote Difference, 2000–2012

Year	*Democrats*	*Republicans*
2000	2,186,190	2,351,209
2004	2,741,167	2,859,768
2008	2,940,044	2,677,820
2012	2,827,709	2,661,437
Total	10,695,110	10,540,234

Total Votes cast = 21,235,344

Difference = 154,876

Percentage Difference = .7 percent

Data source: "Election Results," Ohio Secretary of State, accessed October 4, 2014, http://www.sos.state.oh.us/sos/elections/Research/electResultsMain.aspx

another way, if a candidate is popular in Ohio, they are likely to have qualities that will appeal to voters throughout the U.S. Hence, winning Ohio is important not because of the electoral votes gained but because of what it says about a candidate.

TABLE 1.3 Ohio Basic Facts

	Ohio	*United States*
Population	11.5 million	316.1 million
Female	51.1%	50.8%
White	83.%	77.7%
Black	12.5%	13.2%
Asian	1.9%	5.3%
Hispanic	3.4%	17.1%
High School Graduate	88.2%	85.7%
College Graduate	24.7%	28.5%
Per Capita Income	$25,857	$28,051
Below Poverty Line	15.4%	14.9%

Data source: "State & County QuickFacts," United States Census Bureau, http://quickfacts.census.gov/qfd/states/39000.html

Purple State Politics

More than 50 years ago, Thomas A. Flinn, a political science professor at Oberlin College, wrote an often-cited article describing Ohio politics.[5] Reading that article today, it is remarkable how much of what Flinn documented in 1960 remains unchanged. Flinn concluded, for example, that "Ohio is now and has long been a competitive two-party state in which Republicans have an advantage."[6] He based this statement on the partisan results in presidential, gubernatorial, and state legislative elections in Ohio from 1895 through the 1958 election. Using these same data points for the years beginning in 1960, one finds similar results. From 1895 to 1958, Flinn found that Republicans won 10 presidential elections while Democrats came out ahead in six contests. From 1960 through 2012, the numbers are almost exactly the same, with Ohio voters giving a plurality of their support to Republicans in a little more than half (8) of the 14 contests. Gubernatorial elections, however, tell a slightly different story. By a count of 19 to 12, Flinn's study found that Democrats were more successful than Republicans. Beginning in 1962, however, Republicans reversed the trend and won ten out of the next 15 gubernatorial elections. These increasing gains for Republicans are also reflected in the state legislature. Flinn found that, in the Ohio senate, Republicans held a majority 21 times, while eight senate elections were favorable to Democrats. The senate was tied twice (something that could not happen after 1967, when the size of the senate was set at 33, an odd number). The Republican trend in the senate became even more exaggerated after 1960, with Democrats controlling the senate after only four of 28 elections held through 2014. Where Flinn had found the house "somewhat more Republican than the Senate," the results from 1960 do not bear this out. Unlike in the senate, in the house, Republicans held only a slight edge, maintaining a majority after 16 elections with Democrats capturing the house in the remaining 12 elections.

The end result is that Ohio is a state that leans Republican in state races but tends to give its votes almost equally to Republicans and Democrats in presidential contests. It is this latter fact that gives Ohio its purple state identity. Even this statement, however, must be qualified. For when one looks at the election results tallied by each of the state's 88 county boards of elections, one does not find many purple results. Instead, one finds counties that are consistently deeply red (Republican) and others that are equally as blue (Democratic). Over the years, analysts have come up with various templates to try to both categorize and explain the different voting patterns found throughout the state.

The Rural-Urban Divide

One consistent and obvious distinction is between rural and urban areas. Parts of Ohio that are more densely populated gravitate toward Democrats, while less populated areas tend to support Republicans. In addition, however, economic history and past migration patterns also seem to influence present-day voting. For example, the strong Republican leanings of the southwestern part of Ohio have been linked to the fact that early settlers to the area were antislavery Southerners from Virginia and elsewhere whose descendants gravitated to the Republican Party.[7] At the same time, the fact that northeast Ohio was once the home to large unionized manufacturing facilities helps to explain the strong and consistent Democratic vote found in these counties.

Map 1.2 The Five Ohios

Source: "Basic Information on Ohio Politics #2: The "Five Ohios," Ray C. Bliss Institute of Applied Politics, The University of Akron, accessed October 4, 2014, http://www.uakron.edu/bliss/research/biop-2-the-five-ohios.dot

The Five Ohios

Perhaps the most popular way of understanding the diverse politics of Ohio is to divide Ohio up into five regions. This "Five Ohios" approach identifies the distinct political orientations of northeast, northwest, southeast, southwest, and central Ohio (see Map 1.2). Northeast Ohio is the most Democratic region in the state. Historically, the Democrats' strength in this corner of state is countered by strong Republican voting in the opposite corner of the state, in southwest Ohio. The northwest, central, and southeast regions of the state tend to be more competitive, although the first two regions have leaned toward Republicans.

Curiously enough—and yet another possible reason behind Ohio's identity as a political bellwether—the five regions correspond well to identifiable regions within the nation as a whole. As a paper put out by the Bliss Institute of Politics at the University of Akron explains,

> Northeast Ohio resembles the country's Northeast region in relative terms when it comes to the African American population, population of European ethnicity, and the proportion of Catholics. In contrast, Southeast Ohio resembles the South in terms of poverty and the percentage of Evangelical Protestants. Central Ohio resembles the West in terms of professional/managerial occupations and college degrees. Meanwhile, Northwest and Southwest Ohio resemble the Midwest region as a whole.[8]

As one looks at the results of the most recent presidential races in Ohio, however, the Five Ohios approach seems to be breaking down. Hamilton County, the largest county in southwest Ohio, supported the Democratic candidate Barack Obama in both 2008 and 2012. Southeast Ohio, however, seems to be becoming much more Republican. In 2012, only Athens County (home of Ohio University) supported the reelection of Barack Obama. It is becoming evident that the rural-urban division is still the best way to explain the partisan vote in Ohio. The Democratic candidate, incumbent President Obama, won nine out of the 10 largest counties in Ohio in 2008 and eight of 10 in 2012. John McCain, his Republican challenger in 2008, defeated Obama in nine of the 10 smallest counties. Mitt Romney did a bit better, winning in all 10 of the smallest counties. In fact, Romney won every county in Ohio with a population of under 40,000 residents (27 counties) while losing every county with a population above 500,000 (five counties). (See Figures 1.1 and 1.2.)

Conclusion

Ohio politics have been remarkably consistent over time. Although the state leans Republican, particularly in non-presidential voting, it still roughly follows the mood of the nation. For example, in 2006, as Democrats took over both houses of

FIGURE 1.1 2008 and 2012 Presidential Election Results, 10 Smallest Counties in Ohio

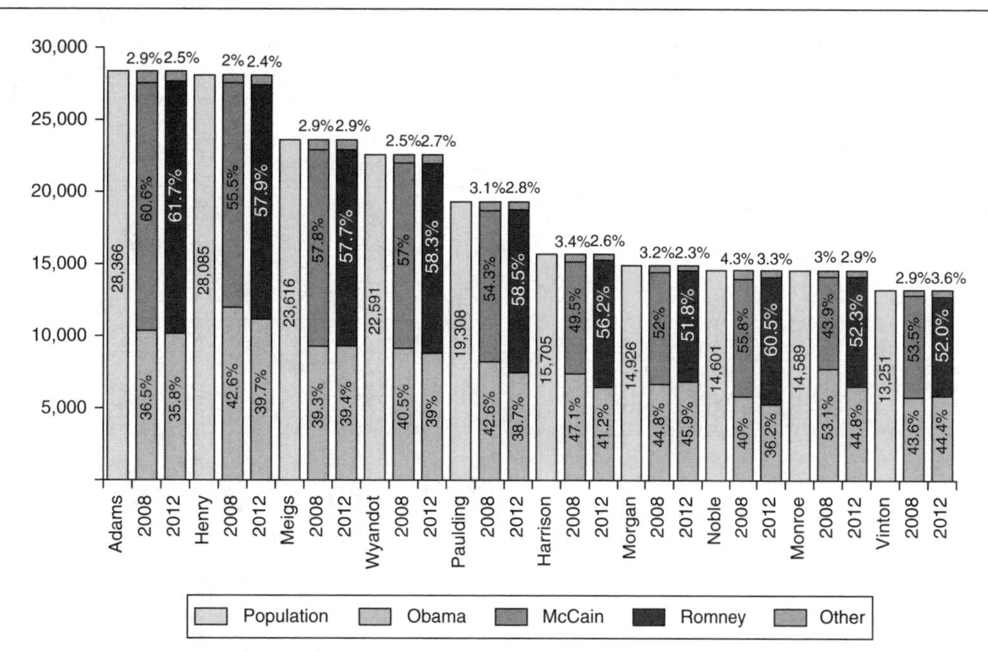

Data source: "Ohio population by County—total residents," US-Places.com, accessed October 4, 2014, http://www.us-places.com/Ohio/population-by-County.htm and "Election Results," Ohio Secretary of State, accessed October 4, 2014, http://www.sos.state.oh.us/sos/elections/Research/electResultsMain.aspx

FIGURE 1.2 2008 and 2012 Presidential Election Results, 10 Largest Counties in Ohio

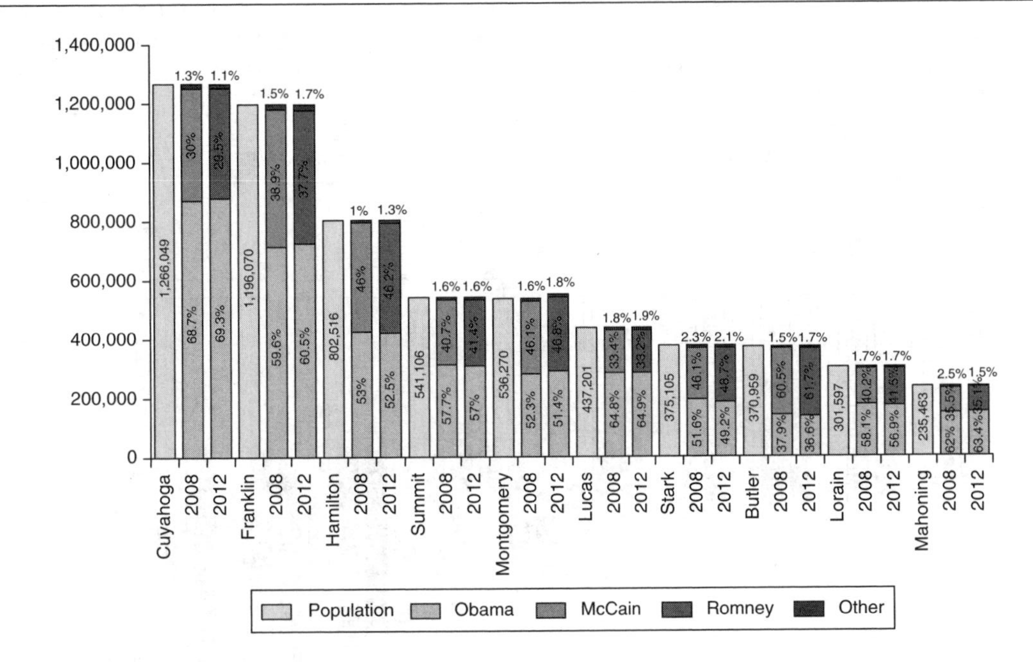

Data source: "Ohio population by County—total residents," US-Places.com, accessed October 4, 2014, http://www.us-places.com/Ohio/population-by-County.htm and "Election Results," Ohio Secretary of State, accessed October 4, 2014, http://www.sos.state.oh.us/sos/elections/Research/electResultsMain.aspx

Congress at the national level, Democrats in Ohio won all but one statewide office. In 2008, Ohio not only supported the Democrat Barack Obama for the White House but also gave his party a majority in Ohio house of representatives. As the nation swung in a more Republican direction in 2010 and 2014, Ohio followed, electing Republicans to every statewide office (in 2010 and 2014) and taking back control of the house of representatives (in 2010). In 2012, Ohio again followed the rest of the country, giving its support to President Obama, but by a smaller margin than it had four years earlier. As we approach the 2016 campaign, only one thing is certain: All eyes will once again be on the Buckeye state.

Notes

1. Oliver Burkeman, "My Fellow Non-Americans," *The Guardian*, October 12, 2004, accessed October 4, 2014, http://www.theguardian.com/world/2004/oct/13/uselections2004.usa11
2. Andy Bowers, "Dear Limey Assholes . . . A Crazy British Plot to Swing Ohio to Kerry,—and How It Backfired." *Slate*, November 4, 2004, accessed October 14, 2014, http://www.slate.com/articles/news_and_politics/politics/2004/11/dear_limey_assholes_.html
3. Jerry Markon and Alice Crites, "Obama Showering Ohio with Attention and Money," *Washington Post*, September 25, 2012, accessed October 4, 2014, http://www.washingtonpost.com/politics/decision2012/obama-showering-ohio-with-attention-and-money/2012/09/25/8ab15a68-019e-11e2-b260-32f4a8db9b7e_story.html
4. California was once considered a competitive state, and some analysts suspect that as its percentage of Hispanic voters increases, Texas will lose its status as a solid red state.
5. Thomas A. Flinn, "The Outline of Ohio's Politics," *Western Political Quarterly* 13 (1960): 702–721.
6. Ibid., 702.
7. John H. Fenton, *Midwest Politics* (New York: Holt, Rinehart and Winston, 1966), 118.
8. "Basic Information on Ohio Politics #2: The Five Ohios," Ray C. Bliss Institute of Applied Politics, The University of Akron, accessed October 4, 2014, http://www.uakron.edu/bliss/research/biop-2-the-five-ohios.dot

Chapter 2

A Brief History of Ohio

Ohio's Path to Statehood

Although Ohio's identity as a battleground state is based on its assumed status as a must-win state for both major political parties in presidential contests, the term might also be understood in a more literal sense: The area that would eventually comprise the state of Ohio was the proximate cause of a real war that indirectly contributed to the establishment of the United States as an independent nation.

Michael Barone and Richard Cohen have suggested that Ohio might rightfully be called the "first entirely American state," since it was the first state with no direct connection to one of the former British colonies.[1] Ohio was never a separate colony under British rule but was part of a disputed area known as the Northwest Territory (Figure 2.1). Bounded roughly by Pennsylvania, the Ohio and Mississippi rivers, and the Great Lakes, the Northwest Territory would eventually give birth to six states, with Ohio being the first.[2] The area boasted of fertile lands and abundant wildlife and was therefore prized by the European powers, particularly Britain and France. In 1749, King George II granted a charter to a Virginia group known as the Ohio Company for lands south of the Ohio River.[3] Although this area was technically not part of the Northwest Territory, it did involve lands claimed by France. The eventual response by France culminated in 1755 with the French and Indian War or Seven Years' War. The Treaty of Paris, which formally ended the conflict in early 1763, gave the British title to the Northwest Territory. Possession passed to the newly freed colonies at the conclusion of the American Revolution.

Northwest Ordinance

In the aftermath of the Revolutionary War, it was difficult to determine which, if any, of the 13 newly independent states actually controlled the Northwest Territory.

FIGURE 2.1 Map of the Northwest Territory

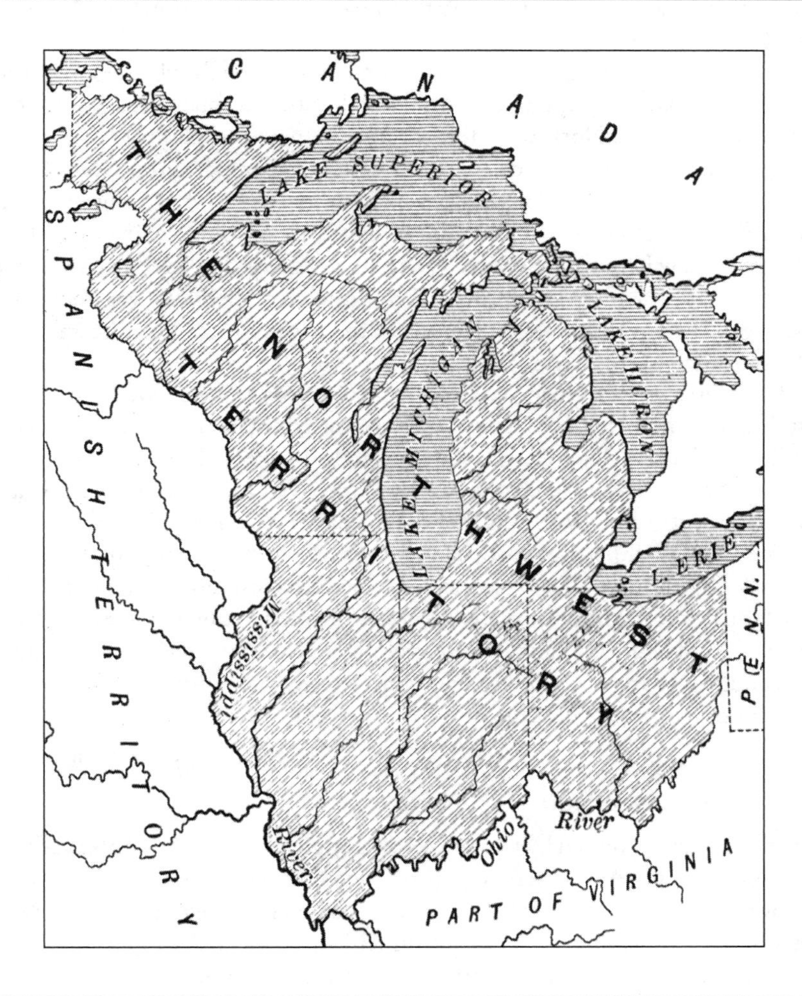

Source: Edward Eggleston, *The Household History of the United States and Its People* (New York: D. Appleton and Company, 1898). Downloaded from Maps ETC, http://etc.usf.edu/maps.

The original British charters establishing the colonies extended their dominion to undefined and as yet unclaimed territories to the west. Arguably, Virginia, New York, and Connecticut could all claim portions of the Northwest Territory and the land that would become Ohio. In fact, as noted in Chapter 1, citizens from all of these states would end up populating this area, and the regions where they settled still influence the political geography of Ohio.

The ratification of the Articles of Confederation, the first U.S. Constitution, was initially delayed by the question of whether the various states would forego their claims over the Northwest Territory to the new central government.[4] This matter was eventually resolved, and the Articles of Confederation Congress took control of the lands. The Congress passed laws in 1784 and 1785 attempting to apportion out the territory and establish a path to statehood. Finally, in July of 1787, as the new U.S. Constitution was being drafted in Philadelphia, the Articles of Confederation Congress approved "An Ordinance for the Government of the Territory of the United States Northwest of the River Ohio." This became known as the Northwest Ordinance (Figure 2.2).

The Northwest Ordinance called for the territory to be divided into "not less than three nor more than five States," with the three initial states called the Western, Middle, and Eastern. The Eastern state was to lie between the Ohio River and the Canadian border, bounded on the east by Pennsylvania and on the west by a line "drawn due north from the mouth of the Great Miami [river]."[5]

The Ohio Company of Associates, a Boston-based company formed about a year earlier by Revolutionary War veterans, had been attempting to purchase land in the Northwest Territory from the Articles of Confederation Congress; two weeks after the Northwest Ordinance was passed, Congress approved the sale.[6] This was the beginning of the large-scale migration of former colonists into the area that would become the state of Ohio.

From a Territory to a State

Five officials, all appointed by Congress, initially governed the Northwest Territory. In addition to a governor, there were three judges and a secretary. Acting together, the governor and the three judges formed a four-member legislature. The Northwest Ordinance mandated the establishment of an elected legislature once the population of free males in a territory exceeded five thousand.[7] By 1798, the governor of the territory, Arthur St. Clair, determined that the population was sufficiently large, and voters were asked to choose members to their first elected territorial legislature.[8]

When the new legislature convened in 1799 in Cincinnati (it would move to Chillicothe in 1800), it consisted of an elected house of representatives and a five-member appointed Legislative Council. One of the first tasks for the new legislature was to select a nonvoting delegate to represent the territory in the U.S. Congress. Given Ohio's later role in selecting presidents, it is perhaps fitting that they choose a future president, William Henry Harrison. Of course, Harrison was

FIGURE 2.2 Northwest Ordinance of 1787

An ORDINANCE for the GOVERNMENT of the TERRITORY of the UNITED STATES, North-Weſt of the RIVER OHIO.

BE IT ORDAINED by the United States in Congreſs aſſembled, That the ſaid territory, for the purpoſes of temporary government, be one diſtrict; ſubject, however, to be divided into two diſtricts, as future circumſtances may, in the opinion of Congreſs, make it expedient.

Be it ordained by the authority aforeſaid, That the eſtates both of reſident and non-reſident proprietors in the ſaid territory, dying inteſtate, ſhall deſcend to, and be diſtributed among their children, and the deſcendants of a deceaſed child in equal parts; the deſcendants of a deceaſed child or grand-child, to take the ſhare of their deceaſed parent in equal parts among them: And where there ſhall be no children or deſcendants, then in equal parts to the next of kin, in equal degree; and among collaterals, the children of a deceaſed brother or ſiſter of the inteſtate, ſhall have in equal parts among them their deceaſed parents ſhare; and there ſhall in no caſe be a diſtinction between kindred of the whole and half blood; ſaving in all caſes to the widow of the inteſtate, her third part of the real eſtate for life, and one third part of the perſonal eſtate; and this law relative to deſcents and dower, ſhall remain in full force until altered by the legiſlature of the diſtrict. ——— And until the governor and judges ſhall adopt laws as herein after mentioned, eſtates in the ſaid territory may be deviſed or bequeathed by wills in writing, ſigned and ſealed by him or her, in whom the eſtate may be, (being of full age) and atteſted by three witneſſes; —— and real eſtates may be conveyed by leaſe and releaſe, or bargain and ſale, ſigned, ſealed, and delivered by the perſon being of full age, in whom the eſtate may be, and atteſted by two witneſſes, provided ſuch wills be duly proved, and ſuch conveyances be acknowledged, or the execution thereof duly proved, and be recorded within one year after proper magiſtrates, courts, and regiſters ſhall be appointed for that purpoſe; and perſonal property may be transferred by delivery, ſaving, however, to the French and Canadian inhabitants, and other ſettlers of the Kaskaskies, Saint Vincent's, and the neighbouring villages, who have heretofore profeſſed themſelves citizens of Virginia, their laws and cuſtoms now in force among them, relative to the deſcent and conveyance of property.

Be it ordained by the authority aforeſaid, That there ſhall be appointed from time to time, by Congreſs, a governor, whoſe commiſſion ſhall continue in force for the term of three years, unleſs ſooner revoked by Congreſs; he ſhall reſide in the diſtrict, and have a freehold eſtate therein, in one thouſand acres of land, while in the exerciſe of his office.

There ſhall be appointed from time to time, by Congreſs, a ſecretary, whoſe commiſſion ſhall continue in force for four years, unleſs ſooner revoked, he ſhall reſide in the diſtrict, and have a freehold eſtate therein, in five hundred acres of land, while in the exerciſe of his office; it ſhall be his duty to keep and preſerve the acts and laws paſſed by the legiſlature, and the public records of the diſtrict, and the proceedings of the governor in his executive department; and tranſmit authentic copies of ſuch acts and proceedings, every ſix months, to the ſecretary of Congreſs: There ſhall alſo be appointed a court to conſiſt of three judges, any two of whom to form a court, who ſhall have a common law juriſdiction, and reſide in the diſtrict, and have each therein a freehold eſtate in five hundred acres of land, while in the exerciſe of their offices; and their commiſſions ſhall continue in force during good behaviour.

The governor and judges, or a majority of them, ſhall adopt and publiſh in the diſtrict, ſuch laws of the original ſtates, criminal and civil, as may be neceſſary, and beſt ſuited to the circumſtances of the diſtrict, and report them to Congreſs, from time to time, which laws ſhall be in force in the diſtrict until the organization of the general aſſembly therein, unleſs diſapproved of by Congreſs; but afterwards the legiſlature ſhall have authority to alter them as they ſhall think fit.

The governor for the time being, ſhall be commander in chief of the militia, appoint and commiſſion all officers in the ſame, below the rank of general officers; all general officers ſhall be appointed and commiſſioned by Congreſs.

Previous to the organization of the general aſſembly, the governor ſhall appoint ſuch magiſtrates and other civil officers, in each county or townſhip, as he ſhall find neceſſary for the preſervation of the peace and good order in the ſame: After the general aſſembly ſhall be organized, the powers and duties of magiſtrates and other civil officers ſhall be regulated and defined by the ſaid aſſembly; but all magiſtrates and other civil officers, not herein otherwiſe directed, ſhall, during the continuance of this temporary government, be appointed by the governor.

For the prevention of crimes and injuries, the laws to be adopted or made ſhall have force in all parts of the diſtrict, and for the execution of proceſs, criminal and civil, the governor ſhall make proper diviſions thereof---and he ſhall proceed from time to time, as circumſtances may require, to lay out the parts of the diſtrict in which the Indian titles ſhall have been extinguiſhed, into counties and townſhips, ſubject, however, to ſuch alterations as may thereafter be made by the legiſlature.

So ſoon as there ſhall be five thouſand free male inhabitants, of full age, in the diſtrict, upon giving proof thereof to the governor, they ſhall receive authority, with time and place, to elect repreſentatives from their counties or townſhips, to repreſent them in the general aſſembly; provided that for every five hundred free male inhabitants there ſhall be one repreſentative, and ſo on progreſſively with the number of free male inhabitants, ſhall the right of repreſentation increaſe, until the number of repreſentatives ſhall amount to twenty-five, after which the number and proportion of repreſentatives ſhall be regulated by the legiſlature; provided that no perſon be eligible or qualified to act as a repreſentative, unleſs he ſhall have been a citizen of one of the United States three years and be a reſident in the diſtrict, or unleſs he ſhall have reſided in the diſtrict three years, and in either caſe ſhall likewiſe hold in his own right, in fee ſimple, two hundred acres of land within the ſame:---Provided alſo, that a freehold in fifty acres of land in the diſtrict, having been a citizen of one of the ſtates, and being reſident in the diſtrict; or the like freehold and two years reſidence in the diſtrict ſhall be neceſſary to qualify a man as an elector of a repreſentative.

The repreſentatives thus elected, ſhall ſerve for the term of two years, and in caſe of the death of a repreſentative, or removal from office, the governor ſhall iſſue a writ to the county or townſhip for which he was a member, to elect another in his ſtead, to ſerve for the reſidue of the term.

The general aſſembly, or legiſlature, ſhall conſiſt of the governor, legiſlative council, and a houſe of repreſentatives. The legiſlative council ſhall conſiſt of five members, to continue in office five years, unleſs ſooner removed by Congreſs, any three of whom to be a quorum, and the members of the council ſhall be nominated and appointed in the following manner, to wit: As ſoon as repreſentatives ſhall be elected, the governor ſhall appoint a time and place for them to meet together, and, when met, they ſhall nominate ten perſons, reſidents in the diſtrict, and each poſſeſſed of a freehold in five hundred acres of land, and return their names to Congreſs; five of whom Congreſs ſhall appoint and commiſſion to ſerve as aforeſaid; and whenever a vacancy ſhall happen in the council, by death or removal from office, the houſe of repreſentatives ſhall nominate two perſons, qualified as aforeſaid, for each vacancy, and return their names to Congreſs; one of whom Congreſs ſhall appoint and commiſſion for the reſidue of the term; and every five years, four months at leaſt before the expiration of the time of ſervice of the members of council, the ſaid houſe ſhall nominate ten perſons, qualified as aforeſaid, and return their names to Congreſs, five of whom Congreſs ſhall appoint and commiſſion to ſerve as members of the council five years, unleſs ſooner removed. And the governor, legiſlative council, and houſe of re-

Source: National Archives, http://www.archives.gov/legislative/images/northwest-ordinance-1.jpg

not a full-fledged member of Congress because Ohio was not yet a state. In fact, one of the major issues to be addressed by the general assembly involved whether the territory should petition Congress for statehood.

Even at this early stage in our nation's history, the area that was to become Ohio was directly tied to national political struggles. The two major political parties at the time, the Federalists and the Republicans, were divided on the question of statehood for Ohio. Both parties suspected Ohio would be a Republican state, and if it became a state, it would increase the power of the Republicans in Congress. As a result, the Federalists, led by Governor St. Clair, wanted Ohio to remain a territory. The governor and his allies in the general assembly did everything in their power to delay the Republican Party's push for statehood. In 1800, Congressional Republicans took the first step toward statehood for Ohio by passing a law dividing the Northwest Territory into two sections, with the eastern division encompassing the area that would become Ohio. In response, Governor St. Clair convinced the general assembly to pass a law dividing the Territory into three districts.[9] None of the districts would have the minimum population of 60,000 required by the Northwest Ordinance prior to consideration for statehood. Congress, however, rejected the division. This set the stage for Ohio to become the 16th state.

In the spring of 1802, the Congress passed a resolution authorizing the inhabitants of the eastern division of the Northwest Territory to form a state government, allowing that once such a government was formed, it would be "admitted to the Union upon the same footing as the original states." In response, the general assembly convened a convention to draft a state constitution. Elections were held in October, and on November 1, 1802, the 35 delegates who were elected met in the town of Chillicothe. Twenty-nine days later, they had hammered out a document calling for an Ohio government consisting of a governor, a two-house legislature, and a judicial branch.[10] On February 19, 1803, the United States Congress passed another act in which it acknowledged both the state's constitution and the formation of Ohio's government.

The manner in which the Congress chose to admit Ohio lead to an ongoing debate about precisely when the Territory became a state. The year 1803 is commonly used, based on the February 19 acknowledgment by the Congress. Arguably, however, Ohio became a state in November of 1802, when the state constitution was ratified, thus forming a government for Ohio. This became more than just a point of contention among historians. Since the actual date of admission cannot be specified, one can make the argument that Ohio is not really a state! Because of this, in 1953, a congressman from Ohio, George Bender, proposed a bill retroactively admitting Ohio to the Union as of March 1, 1803. The bill passed both houses of Congress and was signed by President Dwight Eisenhower in the summer of that year.[11]

The Ohio Constitution

The 1802 Constitution

The basic outline and wording of the first Ohio constitution followed closely the outline of U.S. Constitution that had been drafted only 15 years earlier. Even the placing of the listing of rights at the end of the document resembled the federal Constitution, which had seen a Bill of Rights added as a set of amendments a few years after the original document was ratified.

There was, however, one critical sense in which the 1802 Ohio constitution differed from 1787 U.S. Constitution. The U.S. Constitution established a fairly strong executive branch, while the governorship in Ohio would be much weaker. This may have been a reflection of the fact that the 1802 convention was dominated by Republicans, a party that, consistent with the ideas (though not necessarily the later presidential actions) of its leader, Thomas Jefferson, believed strongly in rule by the many and therefore preferred multimember legislatures to a single-member executive. Under the 1802 Ohio constitution, the governor was to be directly elected to a two-year term but, unlike the members of the legislature, was term limited and could not serve more than six years in an eight-year period. More significant was that the Ohio governor was not granted the power to veto legislation. This meant that the general assembly had the final word on laws of the new state of Ohio.

The 1802 constitution provided for a two-house general assembly. Members of the lower house, the Ohio house of representatives, were to be directly elected and were to serve a one-year term. The number of representatives was not determined in the constitution, but the number was to be proportional to the population and, at least until the white male population over the age of 21 exceeded 22,000, could not exceed 36 representatives.

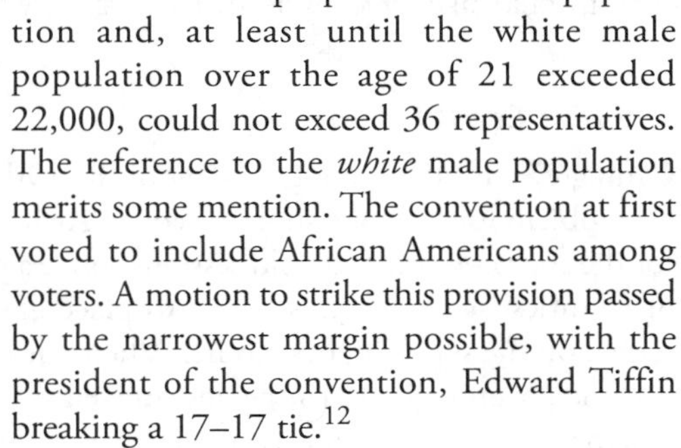
The reference to the *white* male population merits some mention. The convention at first voted to include African Americans among voters. A motion to strike this provision passed by the narrowest margin possible, with the president of the convention, Edward Tiffin breaking a 17–17 tie.[12]

Ohio Historical Society

Edward Tiffin

The house was to share legislative authority with the senate. As was the case with the house, the number of senators was not specified. The only requirement was that the number of senators could not be less than a third nor more than half the total number of members in the Ohio house of representatives. The senators would serve a two-year term, which would be staggered to so that one-half of the senate would stand for election every year.

In addition to passing laws to govern Ohio, the general assembly was to have additional tasks not shared with the governor, including electing the secretary of state, state treasurer, and state auditor. In addition, the two houses of the legislature were to elect the three judges who would form the Ohio supreme court as well as the several judges who would serve on the three courts of common pleas in Ohio.

As already noted, the final article of the 1802 constitution contained a rather extensive listing of rights. Along with protections for freedom of religion and speech and an affirmance of the right to trial by jury, the 1802 document also contained an absolute ban on both slavery and poll taxes. The 1802 constitution concludes with a reminder to the state that "all powers not delegated, remain with the people."

Section 5 of the penultimate article of the 1802 constitution, Article VII, states that any time after 1806,

> whenever two-thirds of the General Assembly shall think it necessary to amend or change this constitution, they shall recommend to the electors, at the next election for members to the General Assembly, to vote for or against a convention, and if it shall appear that a majority of the citizens of the State . . . have voted for a convention, the General Assembly shall, at their next session, call a convention.

It would take Ohioans nearly half a century to avail themselves of this mechanism.

The 1851 Constitution

Ohio grew rapidly in the early days of the 19th century, and this caused a particular problem for the state supreme court. Article III of the 1802 constitution called for the supreme court to hold sessions "once a year in each county." As the number of counties increased, this began to place great burden on the four judges who served on the state's highest court. When one of those judges, Ethan Allen Brown, became governor in 1818, he encouraged the legislature to place the question of whether to convene a new constitutional convention before the voters. The legislature acquiesced, but measure was soundly defeated in 1819 by a vote of 29,315 to 6,987.[13] By the late 1840s, however, with Ohio having expanded to 82 counties, the situation for the supreme court became unbearable. After much political wrangling, the legislature voted on March 23, 1849, to place another call for a constitutional convention before the voters of Ohio. This time, the measure passed by a vote of 145,698 to 51,161.[14]

The convention began its work in Cincinnati on the first Monday in May of 1850. Once again reflecting the national politics of the day, the convention was closely divided politically, with newspapers reporting that about 54 percent of the delegates were Democrats with the rest being Whigs and a handful of Free-Soilers.[15] The convention worked until early July and then reconvened on the first Monday in December before adjourning on March 10, 1851. The constitution that they produced was ratified by the voters in the state of Ohio on June 17 of that year and went into effect about two and a half months later, on September 1.

The 1851 constitution consisted of 16 articles (now expanded to 18). Unlike the 1802 constitution, the 1851 document began with a Bill of Rights that closely tracked the first 10 amendments to the U.S. Constitution. Beyond the addition of a listing of rights, the 1851 document differed in several other ways from its 1802 predecessor. First, the court system was restructured, with the onerous requirement that the supreme court meet annually in each county replaced by a provision that newly formed district courts—consisting of common pleas court judges and one judge from the supreme court—fulfill this mission. The supreme court was expanded to include five judges, and all state judges were to be elected.

In a like manner, the 1851 constitution took the election of the governor, along with the secretary of state, auditor, and treasurer, out of the hands of the Ohio legislature. All of these offices, along with the newly created positions of lieutenant governor and attorney general, would form an executive branch and be directly elected by the people of Ohio. All but the auditor, who was to serve for four years, would be elected biannually. The lieutenant governor would function much like the U.S. Vice President, serving as the president of the Ohio senate while only being allowed to cast a vote in the case of a tie.

Article XVI of the 1851 constitution contained provisions to amend the constitution. There were two basic methods. First, if three-fifths of both houses of the general assembly voted in favor of any proposed amendment, it would be placed on the ballot. Alternatively, two-thirds of both houses of the general assembly could vote to call a convention, which could then "revise, amend, or change" the constitution. Regardless of how these amendments were proposed, they would become part of the constitution if they received support from a majority of voters who participated in the election. This meant that a proposed amendment could receive a majority among those who voted on the amendment yet not be approved because that majority was less than a majority of all those who actually showed up to vote on the day of the election. Finally, beginning in 1871 and every 20 years thereafter, the state was required to place a question on the statewide ballot asking, "Shall there be a convention to revise, alter, or amend the constitution?" If a majority of the voters said yes, a convention would have to be called. Any amendments proposed by a convention, however, would still be subject to approval by a majority of voters.

The 1912 Convention

As required by the constitution of 1851, the question of whether to call a new convention was placed before Ohio voters in 1871. The measure passed, and a convention convened in May of 1873. When the convention finished its work the following May, they had drafted a new constitution as well as several amendments that were tied to the approval of that new constitution. Foreshadowing changes that would eventually be made to the 1851 constitution, the convention's constitution expanded both the number of judges on the supreme court and the term for which they would serve. The governor's office was also strengthened with the addition of a conditional veto.[16] The new constitution was submitted to the voters and was soundly defeated by a coalition that included those who opposed the expanded term for the supreme court judges as well as members of the temperance movement who opposed the amendment on the ballot at the same time that would have allowed for the licensing of alcoholic beverages.[17]

Despite the failure of the 1873 convention, the voters of Ohio did approve 11 amendments to the constitution between 1851 and 1912. Most significantly, an amendment was approved in 1903 that granted the veto power to the governor.

When the required question of whether to call a new constitutional convention was put before Ohio voters in November of 1910, it passed by the extraordinary margin of 693,203 to 67,718. The convention had such strong support because so many different groups—advocating causes from tax reform to women's suffrage to those on both sides of the Prohibition debate—agreed that a convention was needed.[18]

Delegates to the convention were elected a year later, and the convention began its work in Columbus, Ohio, on January 12, 1912. Ohio's importance in national politics was evidenced by the fact that both the current President, William Howard Taft (from Ohio), and former President Theodore Roosevelt visited the convention. Roosevelt, of course, was seeking to wrest the Republican presidential nomination back from Taft, his former vice president. The former president delivered a lengthy and rousing speech in which he emphasized his progressive belief in the initiative and referendum (allowing laws to be voted on directly by the people; see Figure 2.3).

By the end of May in 1912, the convention had agreed to submit 41 proposed amendments to the 1851 constitution to the voters. On September 3, 1912, at a special election, 33 of these amendments were approved. These amendments significantly altered the 1851 constitution by, for example, expanding the membership of the Ohio supreme court and adding a chief justice as well as by altering the governor's power to veto legislation. Most significantly, the people of the state of Ohio would now be able to directly initiate both laws and constitutional amendments as well as challenge by referendum laws already passed by the general assembly. One of the amendments approved in 1912 also made it easier to approve all future amendments.

FIGURE 2.3 Announcement of Roosevelt's Speech at the 1912 Convention

ROOSEVELT STARTS ALONE FOR OHIO

Expected to Outline a Platform in To-day's Speech to the Columbus Convention.

HIS NEXT TRIP TO BOSTON

That, Too, May Have Political Significance—Letter as to His Candidacy Expected Monday.

Col. Roosevelt left for Columbus, Ohio, on the Pennsylvania Railroad at 6:34 o'clock last night, and will arrive in Columbus this morning, when at 11 o'clock he will deliver his address before the Constitutional Convention. This address is awaited with great interest as in it, his friends predict, he will outline his platform. His reply to the letter signed by eight Governors, asking him to define his position, will be made public a few days later, probably by Sunday or Monday. There is little doubt that in this reply he will say that, while he is not seeking the nomination, he will accept if named at the Chicago Convention.

The Colonel spent a quiet day at The Outlook office yesterday, receiving a few visitors, among them Col. William R. Nelson, editor of The Kansas City Star, and John Temple Graves. He refused to comment on the political situation.

Col. Roosevelt went to the Pennsylvania Station unaccompanied. He bought some magazines at the newsstand and talked with the newspaper men for a few minutes. When asked about his Boston trip, on which he will start Saturday afternoon, he said that he did not expect to make any addresses and that he would spend the time with friends there, making calls and talking over old times. Many of Col. Roosevelt's friends, however, predict that the trip will be one of considerable political importance, especially in view of the recent developments in Massachusetts, where a hard fight is already under way to capture the delegation for Col. Roosevelt.

The report was again in circulation yesterday that Roosevelt headquarters will be officially opened early next week in this city, following his reply to the call of the Governors, and that the fight in New York State will then be begun with renewed vigor. Col. Roosevelt had no comment to make on this report.

On his return from Columbus Thursday morning Col. Roosevelt will probably go at once to the home of J. West Roosevelt, at 110 East Thirty-first Street, and may not return to Oyster Bay until after his trip to Boston. He said, however, that he did not expect to make his home in this city permanently, and would probably be at Oyster Bay during the Spring, despite the fact that Mrs. Roosevelt and Miss Ethel Roosevelt will leave Saturday for a trip to Panama that will probably extend over several weeks.

The New York Times
Published: February 21, 1912

Source: The New York Times, "Roosevelt Starts Alone for Ohio," February 21, 1912.

Post-1912 Constitutional Changes

As required by the constitution, the question of whether to call a new constitutional convention has been placed before Ohio voters every 20 years. Since 1912, however, it has failed every time, most recently in 2012. Nevertheless, the Ohio constitution has changed in significant way over the past 100 years. During that period, Ohio voters have approved more than 120 amendments to the constitution, including adding term limits for all state office holders, defining marriage as between a man and a woman, and, in 2010, authorizing casino gambling in the state of Ohio.

Conclusion

From its days as a territory through its movement toward statehood, Ohio been strongly influenced by contemporary political debates. This is nowhere more evident than in the development of the Ohio constitution. The initial constitution, drafted in 1802 as the Jeffersonian Republicans were seizing power from the Federalist Party, reflected Republican fears of concentrated power. When progressive politics captured the imagination of the nation in the early twentieth century, the constitution was altered to allow citizens to directly initiate legislation and constitutional amendments. In the 1990s, when the national mood turned against so-called professional politicians, Ohio joined other states in amending its constitution to limit the number of terms office holders were allowed to remain in a particular position. In 2004, when the subject of same-sex marriage was being debated nationwide, Ohio voters approved an amendment banning the recognition of same-sex couples.

Despite all of the changes and the expansion of the Ohio constitution from its original 16 articles to its present 18 articles, the 1851 document has never been completely replaced. Of course, in about another 20 years, Ohio voters will again be asked if they would like a new convention. In the meantime, House Bill 188, passed by the 129th general assembly and signed into law in the summer of 2011 by Governor John Kasich, established the Ohio Constitutional Modernization Commission. This 32-member commission, which will be in existence until 2022, is charged with "making recommendations from time to time to the general assembly for the amendment of the Constitution."[19] Only time will tell whether all or any of the changes recommended by the Commission will become part of the Ohio constitution. History, however, teaches that whatever changes are adopted, they will likely not be very far out of step with the national politics.

Notes

1. Michael Barone and Richard E. Cohen, *The Almanac of American Politics, 2010* (Washington DC: National Journal Group, 2009), 1155.
2. The states are Ohio, Illinois, Indiana, Michigan, Mississippi, and Wisconsin.
3. Carrington T. Marshall, *A History of The Courts and Lawyers of Ohio* (New York: American Historical Society, 1934), 9.
4. Marshall, 34.
5. The Avalon Project, *Transcript of the Northwest Ordinance* (New Haven: Yale Law School, 1787), http://www.ourdocuments.gov/doc.php?flash=true&doc=8&page=transcript
6. Ibid.
7. Ibid.
8. David M. Gold, *Democracy in Session: A History of the Ohio General Assembly* (Athens, OH: Ohio University Press, 2009), 6.
9. Ibid., 14.
10. G. Alan Tarr, *The Ohio Constitution of 1802: An Introduction* (Rutgers Univ. Center for State Constitutional Studies, 2000).
11. Fred J. Blue, "The Date of Ohio Statehood," *Ohio Academy of History Newsletter* (Autumn 2002): 1.
12. Tarr.
13. Marshall, 94.
14. Ibid., 104.
15. Ibid., 107.
16. "The Proposed Constitution of 1874," in *The Constitutions of Ohio,* ed. Isaac Franklin Patterson (Cleveland: The Arthur H. Clark Co., 1912), 182–236.
17. Barbara A. Terzian, "Ohio's Constitutional Conventions and Constitutions," in *The History of Ohio Law*, eds. Michael Les Benedict and John F. Winkler (Athens, OH: Ohio University Press, 2004), 62–63.
18. Ibid., 63–65.
19. "The Ohio Constitutional Modernization Commission," accessed October 14, 2014, http://www.ocmc.ohio.gov/ocmc/about

CHAPTER 3

The Ohio Legislature

Origins of the Ohio Legislature

The Ohio general assembly originally convened in Chillicothe, the same town that had given birth to the state's constitution, where it remained until 1813. After a brief two-year stay in Zanesville, the legislature moved to its current home in Columbus in 1816 (Photo 3.1).[1]

Using language that was similar to that contained in the Northwest Ordinance, Ohio's first constitution called the legislative branch a *general assembly*, the same name that is used today. This general assembly was to consist of two chambers.

Ohio Statehouse

Both houses of the legislature were to be led by a speaker. Senators were to serve for two years, while members of the house of representatives served for only one year. A staggered election system was adopted for the senate, with one-half of the senators required to face the voters each year. The total number of members of the general assembly could change, and their overall number was linked to the population of the state. The number of senators was also flexible; however, that number could not fall short of one-third nor exceed one-half of the number of house members.[2]

Reflecting the distrust of executive authority of that era, all power was vested in the general assembly. The governor, who was popularly elected, was merely a figurehead, without even the power to veto acts of the legislature. Other state officials, including judges, were selected by the legislature rather than by a popular vote.

The organization of Ohio government remained the same until 1851, when Ohio drafted a new constitution. As already discussed in Chapter 2, this new constitution made several changes to the 1802 document. For example, in addition to the governor, the other executive office holders and judges were now to be chosen directly by the electorate. The legislature was required to meet once every two years, and the terms of house members were lengthened by a year, equaling the two-year term for senators. A Speaker was still to lead the house, but a newly created office of lieutenant governor would preside over the senate. This last change was more of a formality, since, in practice, the president pro tempore would lead the senate.

The Ohio constitution has remained in place since 1851. Nevertheless, many changes have been made to the document through the amending process. Some of these alterations have affected the legislature. In 1903, for example, an amendment was added that granted a conditional veto power (meaning that it can be overridden by the legislature) to the governor. Then, in 1956, the voters of the state of Ohio approved an amendment increasing the term for members of the senate to four years. In 1979, somewhat reversing a change that had been made in 1851, the lieutenant governor was removed as head of the senate, replaced by a senate president. One of the most significant changes, however, has involved legislative districts.

Apportionment

Under the 1851 constitution, there was a very complex formula for the apportionment (or dividing up) of legislative districts. The ratios of population to representation for the house and senate were to be determined by the governor, auditor, and secretary of state acting together, and the formula allowed them to change the number of members for every legislative session. This formula originated long before the United States Supreme Court established the standard of "one person, one vote," and consequently, there was understood to be no constitutional requirement to have legislative districts that were substantially equal in population. Because of the so-called Hanna Amendment, which was added to the state constitution in 1903, each county was guaranteed at least one representative regardless of population. This resulted in a significant overrepresentation (at least relative to population) in the legislature by the state's rural interests, which meant that urban districts had less of a voice than their population might warrant.

The Hanna Amendment later came under scrutiny as a result of United States Supreme Court decision in *Reynolds v. Simms* (1964). This decision required states to apportion voters in both the lower and upper house electoral districts in a way that insured that every individual's vote would have approximately the same weight. In 1967, and after considerable controversy (and one failed attempt),[3] Ohio responded to these Supreme Court decisions by adopting a state constitutional amendment establishing 99 house districts and 33 senate districts (each comprised of three house districts) and mandating that each of the districts be substantially equal in population. This resulted in a more equitable representation of urban interests than had been the case.

The 1967 amendment also created a five-member Apportionment Board, which continues to be responsible for drawing the state house and senate districts. The members of the Apportionment Board are the governor, secretary of state, and auditor of state as well as one person chosen jointly by the Speaker of the house and the leader in the senate of the same political party of the Speaker. The fifth member of the committee must be a person of the major political party of which the Speaker is not a member. This last provision insures that the board has at least one member from each of the two major political parties.

The Ohio constitution mandates that the Apportionment Board be convened by the governor on a date between August 1 and October 1 in each year ending in a "1" (for example, 1991, 2001, and 2011). Before October 5 of that year, the governor must publish the map drawn by the board. The district map is based on numbers generated by the census taken in the preceding year (for example, 1990, 2000, and 2010).

The power exercised by the Apportionment Board makes the election for the statewide executive offices that is held directly prior to or during a census year extremely consequential. The two members chosen by the general assembly leaders will always be of different parties; therefore, whichever party manages to win at least two of the three relevant executive offices (governor, secretary of state, and auditor of the state) will also control the Apportionment Board. For example, the Republicans in Ohio gained majority control of this board in 1990 when George Voinovich was elected governor and Bob Taft was elected secretary of state. Although the auditor of the state (Thomas Ferguson) was a Democrat, Republicans outnumbered Democrats on the board 3–2 and were able to draw state legislative districts that were favorable to their party. The Republicans kept control of the governor's mansion and the secretary of state's office in the 1998 election and, by this time, also controlled the auditor's office. This put the Ohio Republicans in the position to once again control the drawing of legislative districts after they were reapportioned in response to the 2000 census. Although Republicans lost nearly all of the statewide offices in 2006 (they held on to the auditor's seat), they rebounded in 2010, just in time to once again hold a clear majority on this board when it came time to draw new districts in 2011. The relationship between total votes cast for the Ohio house and the seats won by each of the parties is shown in Table 3.1.

TABLE 3.1 Ohio House Election Results in 2012

Ohio House Election Results in 2012				
Party	*Total Votes*	*Percentage*	*Total Seats*	*Percentage*
Democrats	2,530,169	51%	39	39%
Republicans	2,430,181	49%	60	61%

Data source: "Election Results," Ohio Secretary of State, accessed October 7, 2014, http://www.sos.state.oh.us/SOS/elections/Research/electResultsMain/2012Results.aspx

The reason that political control of the Apportionment Board is so important is because of a practice known as *gerrymandering*. Political gerrymandering means drawing districts to benefit the election of either a Republican or a Democratic representative. The practice is nearly as old as the republic itself. Indeed, the term *gerrymander* refers to Elbridge Gerry, a late 18th/early 19th century politician who was particularly adept at drawing the oddly shaped districts (one of which looked like a salamander) that often result from these political considerations.

Despite the importance of political gerrymandering, at least since the 1960s, population also matters. The population of election districts has to be substantially equal. In 2012, for example, the ideal size for house districts in Ohio was determined to be 116,530. This number was determined by dividing the state's 2010 population of 11,536,504 by 99, which is the number of seats in Ohio house of representatives. In actual practice, a district's population may vary from a low of 110,704 to a high of 122,356. Further deviation is allowed to avoid dividing a county. For example, Columbiana, Ohio, had a population of only 107,841 but has retained a single Ohio house seat. Senate districts are not drawn separately but simply follow the boundaries of three contiguous house districts (see Map 3.1 for the current state legislative districts).

In December of 2014, the Ohio general assembly overwhelming voted to place a constitutional amendment before the voters that would alter the process for drawing state legislative district lines. If the amendment passes, the Apportionment Board (renamed the Apportionment Commission) will expand from five to seven members, with the two additional members being appointed, one from each party, by the state legislature. This would guarantee that at least two of those serving on the Board would be from the minority party. Any apportionment plan that did not receive at least two votes from the party in the minority on the board could still go into effect, but it would only remain in place for four years, rather than ten years.

This plan would only affect the drawing of state legislative districts. The Apportionment Board does not draw the boundaries for federal congressional districts. Instead the power is given to the general assembly as a whole. During the 2012 congressional reapportionment, the nationalization of Ohio politics was front and center. Ohio's federal delegation shrunk from 18 to 16 as a result of the 2010 census. The Republican-controlled Ohio house and senate had to therefore deal

MAP 3.1 Current Ohio State Legislative District Map

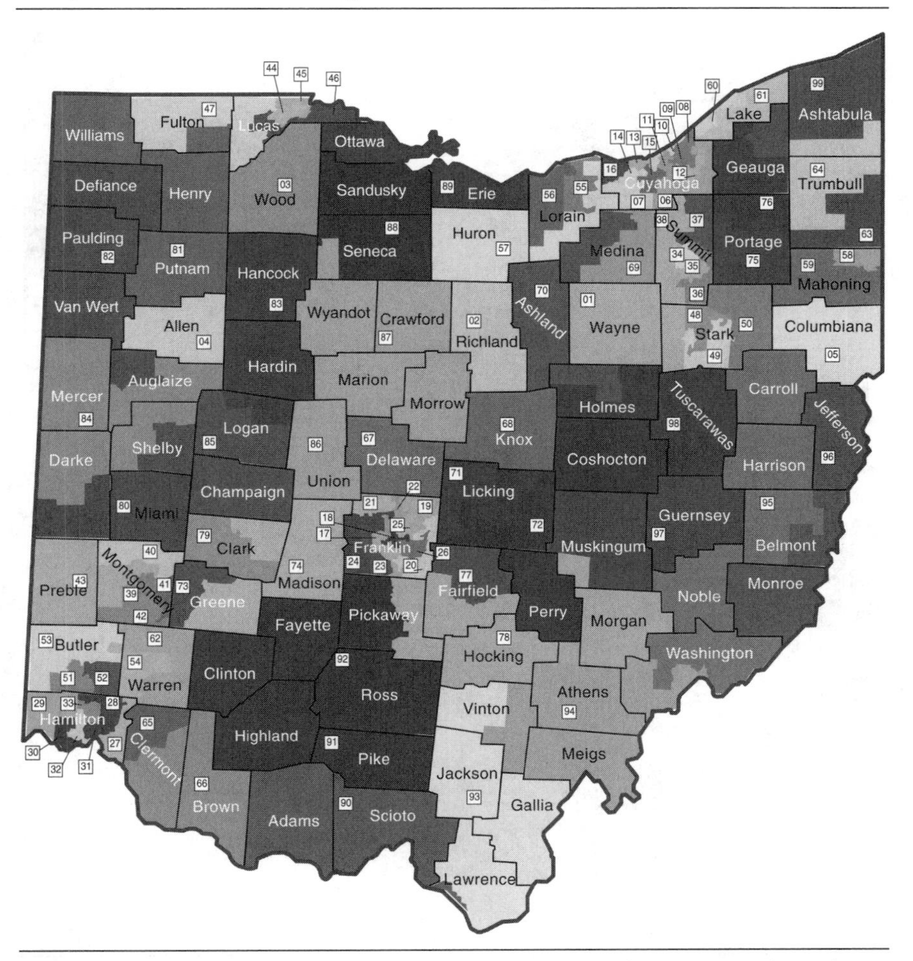

Source: "Ohio House Districts 2012–2022," Ohio Secretary of State, accessed October 7, 2014, https://www.sos.state.oh.us/sos/upload/reshape/GA/Adopted-House.pdf

with the loss of two seats. The map they designed, which sought to lock in as many of the 2010 gains as possible, drew criticism from both Democrats and government watchdog groups. Among the criticisms voiced by Democrat Ron Gerberry (D-Youngstown) on the floor of the Ohio house of representatives was that "[Speaker of the house] John Boehner had more to do with this map than anyone in this room." Nevertheless, because the map created an additional minority-majority district (a district where members of a national minority make up a majority of the population) in the Columbus area, it received the support of some African American Democrats in the legislature (see Map 3.2).

MAP 3.2 Ohio Congressional District Map

Source: "Ohio Congressional Districts 2012–2022," Ohio Secretary of State, accessed October 7, 2014, https://www.sos.state.oh.us/sos/upload/reshape/congressional/Congressional-Statewide.pdf

Candidates and Political Parties

The eligibility requirements are the same for both houses of the Ohio general assembly. Candidates must be at least eighteen years of age and a resident of their district for at least one year. Although convicted felons who have completed their sentences are allowed to vote in Ohio, they are not eligible to serve in the general assembly.

Political parties in Ohio have traditionally played a strong role in recruiting candidates for the general assembly. In competitive districts (districts in which neither party has a significant party registration advantage) and especially in districts where there is an open seat, parties will attempt to recruit attractive candidates. Usually this means that they will try to locate a candidate who either already holds an elective office in the district or is well known and well respected in the area. A number of the legislative districts in Ohio have strong leanings toward one political party or the other. In those districts, the primary will often determine who will represent that district, and the state party will usually refuse to take sides.

Because of gerrymandered districts, the number of competitive seats in an Ohio general election usually does not exceed about two dozen in the house and three to four seats in the senate (since only about half of the 33 seats are on the ballot every two years). Still, control of the houses can hinge on these seats, and in these races, political parties and the interest groups and political action committees (PACs) that are closely linked to the parties will naturally spend heavily. It has been decades since the Democrats had the majority in the Ohio senate; currently outnumbered 23 to 10, it is very unlikely the Democrats will gain a majority in that legislative body anytime soon. The Democrats have been more competitive in the Ohio house. They captured the house after a long draught with a slim majority on Barack Obama's 2008 coattails but lost it in the Ohio Republican tidal wave in 2010. In the 130th general assembly, the number in the house is 61 Republicans to 38 Democrats.

Much of the recruitment and campaign financing activities engaged in by political parties actually take place through what are called *party caucuses*. A party caucus consists of all of the members of a particular political party within one of the two houses of the legislature. So, for example, all of the Republican members of the Ohio house of representatives are known as the Ohio house Republican caucus. These party caucuses are particularly important when it comes to raising campaign funds. The party caucus that holds the majority will generally have more funds than the minority party, since those who seek to influence Ohio government through their donations will naturally give their money to those who actually hold the reins of power.

The party in the majority has a significant advantage in fundraising. Interest groups and favor seekers contribute more often and significantly more money to the party in the majority. Records show that legislative leaders are the top contributors to their caucus finance committees. These leaders know that their continuing tenure depends on their party maintaining control of their chamber and they need to raise the money to retain the majority and keep the support of their caucus members.

As an example of the use of these committee and caucus funds, it is helpful to look at the case of Dan Dodd. Going into the 2010 general election, Dodd was an

Former Ohio Representative Dan Dodd

incumbent Democratic house member who was seen as vulnerable (he did, in fact, lose his seat). His race was therefore targeted by the Ohio house Democratic caucus. He received $541,090 from the house Democratic Caucus fund of Ohio and an additional $201,896 from the Ohio Democratic Party. In the end, in the battle over just one of 99 available house seats, the total spent on Dodd reached $1,053,907. The lion's share of those funds came from Democratic Party committees and caucuses.

Because of the amount of money often spent on Ohio legislative races, it is imperative that party leaders see to it that their party caucus raises the funds, recruits the candidates, and targets those races that will retain the control of the majority. For better or worse, this has made successful fundraising one of the major steps on the ladder of success that must be climbed by those aspiring to be leaders in the legislature in Ohio.

Demographics

The percentage of women in the Ohio legislature has held relatively steady at slightly over 20 percent since the early 1990s. It dropped below 20 percent in the 127th general assembly (2007–2008) but has since increased. In the 130th general assembly (2013–2014), there are 28 women (21 percent of the total) and 103 males. Overall, the percentage of women in the senate is higher than the percentage of women in the house.[4]

There is significant variation in the age of members. The 129th general assembly (2011–2012) had 50 members who were between the ages of 18 and 29, while only four were older than 56. A majority of the members (70) were between the ages of 30 and 55.

In terms of race, there are currently 15 African Americans serving in the general assembly. Ten African Americans serve in the Ohio house, while five hold senate seats. African American legislators are organized as the Ohio Black Caucus. The Ohio Black Caucus has been able to wield significant influence in the Democratic legislative caucus, often capturing prized committee seats. Although all of the African American members of the legislature are Democrats, the caucus has been politically savvy, sometimes forming coalitions with Republicans on issues that are seen as beneficial to their voters. The caucus has historically been very effective at achieving its legislative goals. African Americans serve as the minority leaders in both the house and the senate in the 130th general assembly.

Legislative Term

Each general assembly in Ohio lasts for two years and is divided into two sessions. Taken together, these two sessions are referred to collectively as the *biennial session* of the Ohio general assembly. The first session begins on the first Monday in January of odd-numbered years, provided that the Monday is not a holiday. Legislation may be carried over from the first session into the second session. Any proposed bills that are not completed by the end of the second session, however, must be reintroduced in the next general assembly in order to be considered.

Legislative Vacancies

If a member dies or resigns from their seat during their term in office, the vacancy is filled by a resolution of the members of that particular house who are also members of the same political party as the individual whose seat has become vacant. So if a house member who is a Democratic resigns, a majority of Democrats in the house will be allowed to name someone (presumably another Democrat) to fill the vacancy. In the house of representatives, this newly appointed member will hold the seat for the remainder of the term. In the senate, where the term is longer, if the member who has vacated their seat served less than 20 months of their term, then whoever is appointed (if they want to remain in the seat) must stand in the next general election to fill the remainder of the four-year term. The benefit of being appointed (provided one wins reelection) is that the years served as an appointee do not count toward the term limit of eight years. Of course, being an appointee also enhances the likelihood of success when it comes time to actually run for the seat. In the 129th general assembly, 19 members were appointed to vacated house seats and nine were appointed in the senate.[5] This unusually high number was accounted for by Republican legislators taking positions in the Kasich administration. These appointments give advantages to the newly appointed incumbents in developing constituency relations, fundraising, and increasing name identification.

One question in the study of state legislators is whether the position is full time or part time. A recent history of the Ohio general assembly written by David M. Gold asserts, "A theme that runs throughout this work is the transformation of the General Assembly from a part-time body of citizen lawmakers into a full-time professional legislature."[6] Perhaps it is more accurate to say the job of an Ohio legislator is their primary occupation. For some Ohio state legislators, it is their full-time job. Others maintain some other type of employment. The base salary of a member of the Ohio general assembly is $60,584. That comes with health insurance and state retirement benefits. Those in positions of leadership receive higher salaries. The Speaker and the president of the senate receive a salary of $94,437. Committee chairs and ranking minority members receive quite modest supplemental pay ranging from $2,500 to $10,000. It is quite likely many of those are full-time positions by choice. Many members do try to maintain other occupations. For example, Robert Hagan (D-Youngstown), a longtime member of the Ohio legislature, was able to retain his job as a railroad engineer. Many of the legislators are lawyers, and they maintain a law practice. A normal week when the legislature is in session for a member is to go to Columbus on Tuesday and leave on Wednesday or Thursday, depending on committee assignments. The work of the member is intermittent. They are very busy on odd-numbered years, when the biennial budget is considered. They meet almost every week from January to the end of June. They are in session in the fall, but not for long in even-numbered years when they are standing for election. Of course, legislative sessions and committee work are not all that Ohio state legislators have to do. They have meetings with lobbyists and constituent requests for services. They have meetings and events in the district and attempt to maintain visibility in their home district.

Powers and Structures

Legislative Powers

> The legislative power of the state shall be vested in a General Assembly consisting of a Senate and House of Representatives but the people reserve to themselves the power to propose to the General Assembly laws and amendments to the constitution, and to adopt or reject the same at the polls on a referendum vote as hereinafter provided.
>
> The Ohio Constitution, Article II, Section 1

As the Ohio constitution states, the Ohio house and senate are essentially equal in their legislative authority. Collectively, however, the authority of the Ohio legislature is circumscribed and diluted by constitutional amendments, adopted in 1912, enacting the initiative (used for proposing a law) and the referendum (used for disapproving a law). In fact, there has been a growing trend in Ohio for groups that are dissatisfied with the legislature to attempt to use the initiative and referendum process to either bypass the legislature or to attempt to overturn what the legislature has done.

Of course, the vast majority of lawmaking in Ohio remains the product of the general assembly exercising its constitutional powers. As described by the Ohio Legislative Services Commission in their *Guidebook for Ohio Legislators*, legislative power in Ohio can be divided up into three distinguishable categories.

Political Power

All political subdivisions in Ohio are the creation of the general assembly. Therefore, the legislature has the power to pass laws providing for the organization and authority of county, township, and municipal governments. This power is referred to as *political power*, in part because it is what allows the legislature to establish political offices below the state level. In addition, however, the authority of the legislature to establish and fund administrative agencies with statewide authority would also be included under the concept of political power, as would the responsibility of the Ohio state senate to approve or disapprove of executive appointments that are only to be made with its consent.

A final political power that may be exercised by the general assembly is the power to impeach and remove state officials. The house of representatives can bring articles of impeachment—a set of charges—against an official. In order for this to happen, a majority of the members elected to the house must vote to adopt each article. The house must then transmit these charges to the senate, which determines if the misconduct has, in fact, occurred. A two-thirds vote is required for conviction on any of the articles brought forward, and the person must then resign. The house and senate, by a two-thirds vote, can also decide to remove a judge from office.

Police Power

One of the greatest powers exercised by all state governments in the United States is commonly termed *police power*. Unlike the federal Congress, states are not limited by an enumerated set of powers. While some of these legislative powers may be specifically laid out in the state constitution, others are simply seen as a traditional responsibility of state government. Among the latter would include powers ranging from the authority to determine who is legally able to be married in a state to establishing what the appropriate punishment is for crimes. Also included as a police power is the important state function of providing for and maintaining a public school system. This power over education, however, is specifically mentioned in the Ohio constitution. Article VI, Section 2 states that the legislature must maintain a "thorough and efficient system of common schools throughout the state."[7] Whether or not the general assembly has lived up to this responsibility has been the question at the heart of the many school funding cases that have been heard by the Ohio supreme court over the past few decades.

Taxing Power

When requiring the general assembly to provide for schools, the Ohio constitution explicitly ties this responsibility into another power granted to the legislature: the power to tax. Governments cannot function without revenue, and the Ohio general assembly is charged with raising funds that are sufficient to support the government's responsibilities. Consequently, the legislature has the power to establish new taxes or to raise or lower existing taxes. Historically, Ohio government has been funded in many different ways. For example, the legislature has passed an income tax and a sales tax. The taxing power may be used to achieve a policy outcome as well as raise money. The Ohio cigarette tax is an example of such a measure, since it not only brings money into the state government but also makes a package of cigarettes much more expensive, thereby dissuading people from smoking. Of course, in addition to using taxes to try to turn people away from harmful behavior, the power to raise revenue may also allow the state to profit from behavior that some might find questionable. There has been a tremendous expansion of gambling in recent years in Ohio. The state believes that casino license fees and taxes augment state coffers.

Legislative Leadership and Politics

The 1990s saw a change occurring on the composition and style of legislative leadership in the Ohio general assembly. Brian Usher and Andrew M. Lucker captured the older style of leadership when they wrote that "Moderate legislative leaders and the two GOP governors (Voinovich and Taft) fought to keep their younger, conservative colleagues focused on realistic solutions to state problems as well as single-issue politics and ladder climbing."[8] These authors note that a common tactic used to reign in legislative conservatives—nicknamed the "cave man caucus" by their critics—was to use Democratic votes combined with the votes of moderate Republicans to counter more conservative Republicans.

That leadership approach in Ohio has changed. The new leadership that emerged as a result of the 2010 elections—including the new Republican governor, John Kasich—not only does not seek to reign in the conservatives, as their Republican predecessors had done, but rather have urged them on. By 2012, the Ohio Republicans used their leadership positions in the legislature to help to redefine the Ohio Republican Party in a way that reflected the ideas of the dominant national strain of the party. Although the Republican-dominated legislature maintained their conservative bone fides, Governor Kasich parted ways with his national party and broke with his Republican state legislature by supporting and campaigning vigorously for the expansion of Medicaid to 138 percent of the federal poverty level, which was part of the Affordable Care Act (known as Obamacare) and is an anathema to the conservative wing of the Republicans. Kasich also failed to get many of his tax reforms in his second biennial budget.

Each chamber of the Ohio general assembly has a presiding officer. These officers serve as the leaders for each house. The person in charge of the house of representatives is called the Speaker of the house. In the senate, the presiding officer is known as the president. Although both the speaker of the house and the president of the senate are elected by a vote in which all of the members of their chamber participate, for all practical purposes, each leader is selected by gaining the nomination of their respective party caucus. The caucus that holds a majority of seats in each house will always select their nominee to be the leader by a party line (or near party line) vote. This means that the presiding officers will be committed to retaining their party's majority. The Speaker of the house and the president of the senate wield great power in the legislature; that power, however, will be lost if the majority is lost.

The speaker pro tempore and president pro tempore are second-in-command in their respective houses. In the absence of the presiding officer, they have all the rights, duties, and responsibilities of the presiding officer.

As the heads of their respective chambers, the Speaker of the house and the president of the senate are charged with preserving the order and decorum in their respective bodies as well as with deciding questions of order and procedure. Some of the formal powers of the presiding officers include the following:

1. Recognizing members who wish to speak during floor debates
2. Interpreting and applying the rules of the chamber during floor action
3. Determining the standing committees to be formed in their chambers
4. Appointing members to committees (including the power to replace committee members. In 2011, to insure committee passage of the controversial bill that limited the collective bargaining rights of Ohio public employees, some Republican senators were replaced on the Insurance, Commerce and Labor Committee by the Republican leadership)
5. Acting as chairperson of the all-important Rules and Reference Committee

In addition to these powers, the three top leaders in the house of representatives (the Speaker, minority leader, and speaker pro tempore), while serving as regular members of committees, are also nonvoting members of every other committee. The senate president may substitute as a voting member on any committee. It should be noted that, at times, leadership powers may be assigned by the Speaker or the president to other members. Although it has been customary for the Speaker to chair the Rules and Reference Committee, Speaker William Batchelder assigned the chair position of the Rules and Reference Committee to president pro tempore Matt Huffman and Batchelder served as vice chair.

The main job of the Speaker of the house and the president of the senate is to guide bills through their chamber in the legislature. In fact, these presiding officers are to sign all bills and resolutions enacted by the general assembly to certify that procedural requirements have been met. Of course, the reason that the leadership has this responsibility is to make sure that resolutions and bills produced by the house and senate are consistent with the policies of the leaders' political parties. The party caucuses usually establish these policies (although, when longtime house Speaker Democrat Vern Riffe ruled the Ohio house of representatives, he often did not convene party caucuses). Obviously, a great deal of significant policy making is actually made in the caucus prior to any floor action. This may be seen as problematic to some, since caucus meetings are not open to the public.

Legislative Staff

Legislators no longer share staff (or offices, as they did before the construction of the towering Riffe Center in downtown Columbus). Senators now receive one legislative aide and one secretary for their Columbus office. House members receive only one legislative aide. Legislative research and constituent services are provided out of these offices. The staff who are assigned to these offices are not to be used for campaign activities, which frequently arises as an issue during campaigns. Members do not have district staff nor are they provided district offices. No matter how far outside of the state capital their districts may be located, constituent services must be provided by their staff in Columbus. House and senate committees also have staff assigned to them whose job it is to assist with business that is specific to the subject matter of the committee. When it is time for legislators to draft resolutions, bills, or amendments, they receive support from the nonpartisan Legislative Service Commission.[9]

Committees

A vital part of the functioning of the Ohio general assembly is the committee system. Hundreds of bills are introduced each year by legislators, and committees allow for a division of labor in dealing with what might otherwise be an overwhelming amount of work. Before a bill is ever debated on the floor of either chamber of the general assembly, it must first pass through a committee. This means that, as it is with the federal government, most of the work that is done by the Ohio general assembly is done in committee.

At the beginning of each legislative session, members of the majority and minority parties are queried as to what committee assignments they would prefer. Former Ohio Governor Richard Celeste (D) recalled that, after being on the wrong side of Riffe in Riffe's ultimately successful bid to be reelected as Speaker, Riffe greeted Celeste with "Welcome to the Democratic caucus, and let me know what committees you want to be on. We'll do our best to be fair" (unfortunately, Celeste did not report how that worked out).[10]

Although the Speaker and the president make the committee appointments in their houses, they generally accept the recommendations of the minority leader for minority party membership. By custom, the leadership also acknowledges something known as *proportionality*. *Proportionality* means that the minority receives their proportion of seats on committees based on the percentage of seats that they hold in the legislative body. Current house rules specifically require that committee membership reflect proportionality of partisanship in the house. The presiding officers name the chairs of the committees, and these chairs are always members of the majority party.

All committees may subpoena witnesses to appear before them for the purpose of testifying on legislation. They can also subpoena *duces tecum* (an order to produce books, papers, records, and other evidence). Both houses make an effort to work out committee schedules so that they do not overlap and interfere with members' attendance. The committee chairperson exercises a great deal of authority over the operation of the committee. The chair can determine when the committee meets, which bills referred to the committee will be given a public hearing, the duration of the testimony, and when amendments may be offered.

The rules of the two chambers require that in order to recommend a measure for passage or to postpone further consideration of bills or resolutions indefinitely, the votes of a majority of all the members of the committee must be obtained. A majority of those present is not sufficient.

There are three main types of committees in the Ohio general assembly: standing committees, conference committees, and interim committees. Standing committees, at least in the house, also have subcommittees. Subcommittees are made up of a small number of members of a standing committee and are formed to work on some particular aspect of the overall jurisdiction of the committee. Bills may be referred from the full committee to a subcommittee. Under current rules of the house of representatives, all subcommittees that are not connected to the house Finance and Appropriations Committee may report bills directly to the full house. Nevertheless, as the house is currently organized, only two of the permanent subcommittees would enjoy this privilege.

Standing Committees

Standing committees are the main committees through which potential legislation must pass. Standing committees should schedule hearings, propose amendments, and determine the final form of bills and resolutions. Standing committees, through their action or inaction, may also determine which bills and resolutions will be killed and which will be sent to the floor for debate.

Standing committees are formed at the beginning of each biennial session. It is up to the leadership to determine the number of standing committees, although many of the most important standing committees are simply re-formed in every session. Nevertheless, the number of house committees in the 129th general assembly was reduced from 27 to 17, which was the number in the 130th general assembly.[11] The number of subcommittees in the house is six. The senate has 17 standing committees with three subcommittees of the senate Finance Committee. Table 3.2 below lists the house and senate standing committees in the 130th general assembly.

The jurisdictions (types of subjects they may deal with) of the house and senate standing committees that share the same or similar names do not always overlap. Nevertheless, some standing committees (e.g., the Education and the Finance committees) generally do deal with the same matters.

Rules and Reference Committee

Although the Rules and Reference Committee is technically a standing committee, this committee has quite different functions from other standing committees. In both the house and the senate, the responsibility for assigning bills and resolutions to standing committees is delegated to the Rules and Reference Committees. Introduction of proposed legislation does not always guarantee referral and legislation that is not referred does not go any further in the process. Still, the Rules and Reference Committees do not have complete discretion. In the Ohio house of representatives, for example, all bills introduced before May 15 of the second year of the two-year session must be referred to a committee. In the senate, the date is April 1.

The Rules and Reference Committee plays a role at both the beginning and the end of consideration of legislation. In addition to referring bills and resolutions to other committees, the Rules and Reference Committee schedules floor votes by the full house and senate once bills and resolutions leave committees. The senate Rules and Reference Committee prescribes the order of senate business, arranges the daily legislative senate calendar, and channels all appointments of the governor to the appropriate standing committee before going for senate confirmation. The house Rules and Reference Committee decides which bills and resolutions are on the house calendar.

Conference Committees

If legislation does not pass both houses in the same form and one house cannot be convinced to simply accept the other house's form of the bill, then a conference committee is formed. A conference committee is made up of members from both chambers and is charged with resolving the differences between the two bodies. The usual practice is for three members from each chamber to be appointed to a conference committee.

TABLE 3.2 130th General Assembly Standing Committees

130th GENERAL ASSEMBLY STANDING COMMITTEES	
HOUSE	*SENATE*
Agriculture & Natural Resources	Agriculture
Labor & Technology	Civil Justice
Criminal Justice	Commerce and Labor
Economic Development & Regulatory Reform	Criminal Justice
Education	Education
Finance & Appropriations	Energy & Natural Resources
Financial Institutions, Housing & Urban Development	Finance
Health and Aging	Insurance and Financial Institutions
Insurance	Medicaid, Health & Human Services
Judiciary & Ethics	Public Safety, Local Government & Veterans Affairs
Local Government	Public Utilities
Public Utilities	Reference
Rules & Reference	Rules
State Government & Elections	State Government Oversight & Reform
Transportation, Public Safety & Homeland Security	Transportation
Veterans Affairs	Ways & Means
Ways & Means	Workforce & Economic Development

Data source: "Senate Standing Committees," The Ohio Senate 130th General Assembly, accessed October 8, 2014, http:// www.ohiosenate.gov/committee/senate-standing-committee

Toward the end of a legislative session, as the legislature tries to cobble together bills that can pass both houses and get to the governor's desk, conference committees become very important. In fact, much lawmaking goes on in these committees as amendments are added and language is changed. At times, bills produced by a conference committee can bear little resemblance to the original bills that were supposed to be reconciled. The most notable conference committee is the one formed at the end of the biennial budget cycle where differences are to be reconciled. See Chapter 7 for a discussion of the 2013 conference committee on the budget.

Interim Committees

Interim committees are also called *select committees* and may be composed of members from one or both houses. If members from both chambers are part of the interim committee, it is referred to as a *joint committee*. Interim committees have frequently been used by the legislative leadership to address problems that require more attention than can be allocated in the course of the normal legislative session. A recent effort to establish an interim joint committee to consider racetrack issues was abandoned because it was decided that determining required joint rules for a joint committee would just take up more time, so the houses decided to follow the normal procedure of using regular committees in each house to consider the legislation.

There are a number of permanent joint interim committees. They include the Correctional Institution Inspection Committee, the Joint Legislative Ethics Commission, and the Joint Committee on Agency Rule Review (JCARR). Membership on some joint committees is not restricted to members of the legislative branch. For example, the powerful Controlling Board that, among other things, exercises some important control over the biennial capital budget includes members from the executive branch.

How a Bill Becomes a Law in Ohio

Resolutions and Bills

Public policy can be made by adoption and passage of either resolutions or bills. Resolutions differ from bills in that the former may sometimes be adopted by only one house and do not have to be signed by the governor. There are three different types of resolutions. A simple resolution relates only to matters affecting one house of the general assembly and therefore only needs to be adopted by that house. A simple resolution might involve, for example, the appointment of a leader in a particular house. Joint resolutions and concurrent resolutions are the product of action by both houses. Procedurally, the main difference between a joint resolution and a concurrent resolution is that the secretary of state must sign the former but not the latter. This is because joint resolutions tend to deal with more weighty matters, such as the ratification of amendments to the U.S. Constitution. Concurrent resolutions are used to decide, for example, when the general assembly will adjourn.[12]

All bills, in order to become law, must be passed by both houses of the legislature and certified by the leadership in each chamber. When this happens, a bill officially becomes an act of the general assembly and must be presented to the governor. The governor then has three choices: He or she may veto the act, sign the act, or allow the act to become a law without a signature.

Any member of the general assembly can introduce bills. There are, however, restrictions on types of proposed legislation that may be entertained by the legislature. The United States Constitution prohibits states from passing ex post facto laws, bills of attainder, or laws impairing the obligation of contract. The Ohio constitution mandates that all general laws are to be uniform in operation throughout the state and that no act of the legislature may be dependent upon the approval of any other authority than that of the general assembly. The Ohio constitution also prohibits bills from including more than one subject. The courts have been lenient in allowing the legislature itself to often determine whether or not they are in compliance with this last requirement. In fact, the Ohio supreme court has declared that only a "manifestly gross and fraudulent" violation of the single-subject rule will result in the overturning of legislation.[13] Nevertheless, that court did, in 1999, find a tort law in violation of the single-subject rule.

There are additional areas of the law where the legislature is prohibited from taking action. One example is that the state is prohibited from assuming the debts of any county, city, town, township, or corporation unless the debt has been incurred to repel invasion, suppress insurrection, or defend the state in war. This does not preclude the state from loaning a school district funds. Also, local governments and school districts can come under state control if the state determines that the political subdivision is unable to meet its current obligations. Should they reach this fiscal distress, the state will appoint an oversight board and the local political subdivision loses its authority over financial matters until the fiscal problems are remedied.[14]

Proposing a Bill

The inspiration for a bill may come from a variety of sources. The governor, a state agency, or a state legislator may get an idea for a new law from an interest group, a constituent, or perhaps something that the legislator saw in the news. Regardless of where the notion originated, only a member of the state legislature may actually introduce a bill. Before this happens, however, a legislator takes the idea or proposal to the Legislative Service Commission, a nonpartisan service agency to the legislature, which drafts the bill for the member. This is done to insure that the bill does not conflict with existing language in the Ohio Revised Code. There are many more bills introduced in the Ohio general assembly than actually become law. Table 3.3 below shows the low success rate of bills.

Consideration

The Ohio constitution requires that each bill receive consideration for at least three days in both houses. A two-thirds vote in either house may waive this requirement, but only within that house. The first consideration of a bill consists of a reading of the title of the bill by the clerk on the day the bill is introduced. The bill is assigned a number that it retains for the entire biennial session of the legislature. The more sponsors the bill has, the better its outlook for final passage. The first signature on a bill is by the prime sponsor. If the sponsor is the chair of the committee where the bill is likely to be assigned, that is a good sign that the bill has merit. Opposition can occur at this first reading and a vote may be taken to defeat the bill at this early stage. This, however, seldom happens. The second consideration of a bill occurs when the house or senate Rules and Reference Committee reports back a recommendation for the assignment to a standing committee.

The standing committee will then take up the bill. A major part of the work of a standing committee is to hold hearings to take testimony from those who have a direct interest in a proposed piece of legislation. This is an opportunity for

TABLE 3.3 129th General Assembly

	House Bill Totals	*Senate Bill Totals*
Introduced	623	393
Passed first house	180	108
Passed second house	134	73
Concurrence	131	71
Governor signed	130	71
Law without signature	0	0
Governor vetoed	1	

Data source: "129th General Assembly," Ohio Legislative Service Commission, accessed October 8, 2014, http://www.lsc.state.oh.us/status129/cmte129.pdf

citizens to express their views on a bill and for lobbyists to show their clients that they are working on their behalf. There might be both favorable and unfavorable testimony. Some of the committee members will ask those appearing before them questions about their testimony. Under current rules, the sponsor of the bill is required to appear before the committee at least once. The times and dates of the hearings before committees are public, and notices are posted on the general assembly's website.

The rules of both houses require that committee members be present to vote. Proxy voting, where one member casts a vote for another member, is not allowed. In the case of a scheduling conflict, the roll call on a motion may be held open so that members have an opportunity to cast their vote. A committee can take a variety of actions on a bill. It can report out bills with no changes, adopt amendments, or even offer a substitute bill. Provided that the single-subject rule is not violated, a committee may even combine multiple bills together into a single piece of legislation.

A majority vote is required to either vote the bill out of committee or postpone action indefinitely. The committee report will take note of a situation where significant amendments have been made in committee or if a substitute bill is what is being reported out. A bill that receives a favorable vote will then go to the Rules and Reference Committee of the house or senate.

Floor Action

If the committee approves the bill, the legislation's supporters must work with the appropriate Rules and Reference Committee to get the bill scheduled for floor action.[15] Several considerations may go into when a bill is brought to the floor. Sponsors may want to make sure there are enough votes to pass the bill before it is placed on the calendar. Also, promoters want to be sure to have sufficient time to organize support for the bill before it is scheduled for a vote. At times, other political considerations may come into play.

The house and senate Rules and Reference Committees control access to the floor of their respective chambers. The house or senate Rules and Reference Committee will select from the many bills reported out by committee those that will be scheduled for floor debate and a vote. The selected bill is placed on the calendar of chamber that is debating the legislation. At this point, the bill receives its third consideration. It can be passed, voted down, postponed, or sent back to committee. It should be noted here that a bill that has not been reported out of committee might also make its way to the floor via what is called a *discharge motion*. The motion must be approved by a majority of the house in which the motion is made and cannot be made until 30 days has passed since a bill was referred to the committee.

After a bill has passed the first house, it goes to the second house, where it is subject to the same process. The second house can pass the bill without revisions, amend it, change it, pass a substitute bill, or postpone consideration. If the second house passes a different version of the bill, then it goes to the first house for agreement on the changes. The house that originally passed the bill to which changes have been offered takes up the question of concurrence. They have to vote up or down on the changed bill and cannot offer any revisions. If they concur, the bill passes; if not, the second house can withdraw its changes. If that does not happen, either house—but usually the second house—will call for a conference committee. If a majority of the representatives from each house can agree on a common version of the bill, then a conference report is submitted back to both the house and the senate. The only question posed to the members of both houses in this case is whether to agree to the conference committee report. If either house fails to agree, then the other house is notified and there may be a request for an additional conference committee. If both of the houses agree to the conference report, the bill is enacted. Both the Speaker of the house and the president of the senate are required to sign the bill (now considered an act of the general assembly) before it is sent to the governor. Table 3.3 shows the number of bills introduced and those that became law in the 129th general assembly.

The Governor

The Ohio constitution requires that each act passed by the general assembly be presented to the governor for his or her approval. If the governor signs the act, it becomes law. If the governor fails to sign the act and takes no action for ten days, it also becomes law. Some governors will take this approach to indicate disapproval for an act that they are nevertheless unwilling to veto. Governor James Rhodes took this course of action (or, really, nonaction) when the motorcycle helmet law was repealed in Ohio.

The governor of Ohio can disapprove (or veto) any act of the legislature. In addition, unlike the President of the United States, the Ohio governor has the power to veto particular line items in acts with appropriations. When vetoing a bill, a governor must send it back to the originating house with his or her written objections. That house can vote to override the veto with a three-fifths vote (60 votes in the house and 20 votes in the senate). If one house votes to override, the objections then must go to the second house for the same action. If the override fails in either house, the veto stands. If the law stands, it is filed with the secretary of state.

The Ohio constitution requires that 90 days elapse before a law can go into effect. This delay is linked to right of the people of Ohio to challenge an act of the legislature by placing a referendum on the ballot. The 90-day delay is to allow time for opponents to file the necessary documents and signatures for a referendum. While most acts of the legislature are subject to the referendum, there are exceptions. These include appropriations for the operation of state government and for so-called emergency laws. For an act to follow under the emergency law exception, an emergency clause must be added to the legislation. An emergency clause requires that a separate roll call be taken, and that a two-thirds vote (66 votes in the house, and 22 votes in the senate) be obtained.

Legislative Oversight

In addition to making public policy through passing resolutions and bills, the state legislators serve their constituents by providing oversight over executive branch agencies. The Ohio general assembly uses a variety of tools, including the creation of a number of permanent oversight committees, to watch over the executive branch. One example of such a committee is the Correctional Institution Inspection Committee, which is charged with inspecting private and state-operated adult prisons. The committee can also inspect jails operated by the Department of Youth Services.

The legislature also reviews administrative rules issued by state agencies and has the power to invalidate such rules. This is done through the influential JCARR. JCARR is composed of five members from the house and five members from the senate. Regardless of the makeup of the parties in the legislature, only three JCARR members from each body can be from the same political party. JCARR does not have authority to invalidate a rule, but it can recommend invalidation of a rule to the general assembly.[16]

The Controlling Board also exercises significant oversight. It is discussed in Chapter 7.

A Sunset Review Committee reviews individual agencies according to a fixed schedule. This also serves as oversight, since most agencies will be terminated unless they justify their existence to the legislature and demonstrate that they are carrying out their legislative mandate.

Finally, and perhaps most importantly, legislative oversight is conducted in the biennial budget process, when every general revenue funded agency must go to the legislature for renewed funding.

Current Issues

Term Limits

In 1992, the Ohio general assembly was changed in dramatic fashion when the state's voters approved a constitutional amendment (initiated by the voters) imposing term limits on the members. The voters of Ohio overwhelmingly approved the amendment, with 69 percent of the vote cast in favor of the amendment. According to the amendment, which specified that the clock for the term limits would begin at adoption, house members are limited to four consecutive two-year terms, while senators may serve only two four-year terms. After being term limited out of their chamber, members are allowed to seek a seat in the other chamber. After four years out of a particular house, members can once again return to begin a new two- or four-term cycle. There have been various discussions to repeal or at least lengthen the term of legislators, but those efforts have not materialized into a serious campaign.

Term limits have had a number of effects on the legislature. One obvious result is that there is much less stability within house and senate leadership. Prior to the imposition of term limits, Riffe served nearly twenty years as Speaker of the house. The tenure of leaders since then has been much briefer. Despite this more rapid turnover, it does not appear that the leadership is necessarily weaker nor has there been a great deal of conflict within the majority after the leadership is selected. Recently, for example, the senate and house Republican leaders were able to successfully pass the controversial Senate Bill 5, which would have denied public employees collective bargaining rights. They were also able to muster the votes to pass a very difficult biennial budget in 2011. Still, with term limits, there is a clear loss of institutional memory. There is now a turnover rate in the Ohio legislature of about 30 percent. A majority of this turnover is caused by term limits. It takes about one term for members to become acclimated to the legislative process. With nearly one-third of legislators being new to the job, it is difficult for the leadership to orient all of these new members to their duties.

The high turnover rate also requires the party caucuses to continuously recruit candidates for vacant seats. This places a large burden on party leadership to find talented candidates and to fund their elections. There has been, however, an increase in the number of members elected who have experience in the other house. Therefore, all institutional memory is not lost. The career of house member Ron Amstutz is not uncommon in the Ohio legislature. He served in Ohio House District 3 from 1980 to 2000. Having been term limited out of the house, he moved to the senate in 2001, where he served for eight years. He then returned to the house in the election of 2008. Although he would be counted as a sophomore (serving in the second of his allowed four terms), his knowledge of the legislature, and especially finance matters, is far from sophomoric. His vast experience did not go unrecognized, and he was appointed to serve as chair of the house Finance and Appropriations Committee. He also served on the state Controlling Board, Public Utilities Committee, Legislative Services Commission, and the Ways and Means Committee. Representative Amstutz, nonetheless, remains something of an exception. As result of the strong Republican vote in 2010, many Republicans who were elected to the house had never held any prior public office. More and more, and to a much larger degree than in the past, the Ohio legislature has become a body of strangers.

Term limits in Ohio have also made having a career as a state legislator—once commonplace—less likely. Indeed, this was the intent of the voters. Prior to term limits, if a member came from a "safe district" (i.e., one where the member's party was dominant), they could expect to spend 25 or 30 years in public service prior to retirement. That is now impossible. As we saw with Representative Amstutz, some are able to jump back and forth between the house and the senate to patch together a career. Nevertheless, like Amstutz, many of those who are or were doing this had considerable service before the term limit clock started.

Ohio House of Representatives

Ron Amstutz

Historically, many prominent Ohio political figures started their careers in the Ohio legislature, including former Cleveland mayor, Ohio governor, and then United States Senator Voinovich, and former Secretary of State and former Governor Bob Taft. One of the current United States senators from Ohio, Sherrod Brown, also began his career as member of the general assembly. These individuals, however, may be the exception rather than the rule; seeking higher office is a slippery pole. Political scientist Rick Farmer studied the impact of term limits on the careers of Ohio legislators.[17] He found that 40 percent of house members, and almost half of departing senators, ran for another office. Twenty percent sought election to the other chamber, while 15 percent ran for a local or county office (which might be seen as a promotion if it is a large city or county). About 10 percent of senators ran for Congress. Overall, only about 35 percent of the legislators seeking a different office were successful. Increasingly, a number of legislators take positions with the executive branch if their party controls the office of governor.

Ethics

In 1973, as part of a general nationwide reaction to government corruption, the Ohio legislature passed its first ethics law. The Ohio Ethics Law established a Joint Legislative Ethics Committee (JLEC) and an office of Legislative Inspector General. This is distinct from the Ohio Ethics Commission, which does not have oversight responsibilities over legislators and judges. JLEC has the duty of proposing ethics legislation, which has become much more constraining on legislators over the years. This committee can also initiate, investigate, and hear complaints of alleged misconduct and recommend sanctions for violations. At the beginning of each session, the JLEC recommends a code of ethics to the general assembly. JLEC provides advice to members in the form of both advisory opinions and private written opinions. These opinions are issued in response to hypothetical circumstances, and this allows members of the legislature to gain advice prior to engaging in an activity that might be deemed to violate ethical standards.

Candidates for office, members of the legislature, and certain legislative employees are required to file financial disclosure statements with the JLEC, and there are a variety of prohibitions associated with potential conflicts of interest. In general, members are prohibited from using the authority of their public office to secure anything of value. They also may not solicit or accept anything of value that is of such a character as to "manifest a substantial and improper influence upon a member with respect to the member's duties."[18]

Restrictions on the relationship between lobbyists and legislators are one of the more significant yet continuously evolving areas of Ohio ethics law. Lobbyists in Ohio (referred to as *legislative agents* in Ohio law) are required to register and report spending on legislators. Members of the general assembly who have a business relationship with a lobbyist may not vote on any legislation for those that lobbyist advocates. Where lobbyists were once able to fly legislators to exotic places for such things as golf outings, legislators now may not accept payment from a lobbyist for any travel or lodging expenses. Indeed, a member cannot accept a gift of anything worth more than $75 nor may a member of the general assembly solicit or accept payment (an honorarium) as consideration of a speech given, article published, or attendance at any private or public conference.

Conclusion

While the roots of the Ohio legislature extend back at least to 1787, government in Ohio has evolved over the past 225 years. The size of the legislature has changed, as have the rules for drawing voting districts. Along with apportionment, however, one of the biggest changes to take place in Ohio government has been the imposition of terms limits. As pointed out at the beginning of the chapter, term limits have not only changed the membership of the Ohio legislature, they have facilitated a change in Ohio politics.

Yet term limits are still rather new to Ohio, and the impact is just beginning to be felt. One possible effect will be to weaken the legislature. Should this happen, the power of the governor is likely to increase. Just as increased partisanship in the legislature reflects a national trend, it could be argued that an increase in executive power also mimics what has been seen on the national stage.

Notes

1. Albert H. Rose, *Ohio Government State and Local*, 4th ed. (Dubuque: Kendall Hunt Publishing, 1974), 313.
2. Ibid., 316.
3. Richard G. Sheridan, *Governing Ohio: The State Legislature* (Cleveland: Federation for Community Planning, 1989), 3.
4. Ohio Legislative Service Commission, *A Guidebook for Ohio Legislators* (Columbus: Ohio Legislative Service Commission, 2013), 193.
5. Ibid., 189
6. David M. Gold, *Democracy: A History of the Ohio General Assembly* (Athens: Ohio University Press, 2009), xviii.
7. Steven H. Steinglass and Gino J. Scarselli, *The Ohio State Constitution* (New York: Oxford University Press, 2011), 221.
8. Brian Usher and Andrew M. Lucker, "The Ohio Legislature Since 1994" in *Ohio Politics*, eds. Alexander P. Lamis and Brian Usher, 2nd ed. (Kent: Kent State University Press), 333.
9. Ohio Legislative Service Commission, *A Guidebook for Ohio Legislators*, 89.
10. Vernal Riffe, *Whatever's Fair: The Political Biography of Ohio House Speaker Vern Riffe* (Kent: Kent State University Press, 2007).
11. Ohio House of Representatives, 130th General Assembly Committee Roster.
12. Ohio Legislative Service Commission, *A Guidebook for Legislators*, 47–48.
13. *In re Nowak*, 104 Ohio St.3d 466, 2004-Ohio-6777.
14. Kevin L. Boyce, *Center for Public Investment Management, COMPL 202: What Do We Do Now? A Fiscal Watch and Fiscal Emergency Survival Guide* (2010).
15. Sheridan, *Governing Ohio*, 41
16. Ohio Legislative Commission, *A Guidebook for Ohio Legislators*, 72–73.
17. Rick Farmer and Thomas H. Little, "Legislative Power in the Buckeye State: The Revenge of Term Limits," in *Legislating without Experience: Case Studies in State Legislative Term Limits*, eds. Rick Farmer, Christopher Z. Mooney, Richard J. Powell, and John C. Green (Lanham: Lexington Books, 2007), 43–54.
18. Section 7 ("Improper Influence") in the Legislative Code of Ethics for Members and Employees of the 130th Ohio General Assembly, Employees of Any Legislative Agency, and Candidates for the 131st General Assembly.

CHAPTER 4

The Ohio Executive Branch

The Ohio constitution stipulates, "The supreme executive power of this state shall be vested in the governor." Since 1978, a lieutenant governor has been elected in tandem with the governor. There are four other constitutional executive offices that have defined administrative functions and that are separately elected. This executive fragmentation, however, does not diminish the fact that the Ohio governor is considered a strong governor on measures of formal institutional power.[1] The term of the Ohio governor is four years, with a two-consecutive-term limit. The Ohio governor has appointment powers, a major role in budget making, clemency authority, and a strong veto power that can only be overridden by a three-fifths vote of the legislature.

The effectiveness and strength of the Ohio governor does not rest solely on the constitutional authority of the office. The role of governor is central to Ohio government and politics, and this makes the governor the chief policy promoter and advocate in Ohio. Current Governor John Kasich has been a very active policy initiator compared to the more incremental approach of many of his predecessors. In fact, the only recent Ohio governor who initiated as many significant changes, albeit with a very different policy agenda, was Richard Celeste. Governor Celeste, for example, promoted the public sector collective bargaining law in Ohio that the legislature attempted to alter early on in Governor Kasich's tenure.

The Path to the Ohio Governor's Office

Before 1959, the governor of Ohio was elected to a two-year term every even-numbered year. Ohio voters adopted an amendment in 1954 expanding the term to four years with a two-consecutive-term limit. That amendment went into effect in 1959.

Ohio gubernatorial candidates are not political novices. Most of them are seasoned Ohio state politicians who, with very few exceptions, began their careers in the Ohio general assembly.[2] In some cases, their legislative experience was extensive; two candidates served as Speaker of the Ohio house of representatives. Election to a lower statewide administrative office also has been a common route to the governor's office. On occasion, candidates have gained their party's nomination directly from a local office, usually after being elected as mayor of a large Ohio city. Some of the most notable political figures of the latter part of the 20th century served as big-city mayors. Frank Lausche (D) served as mayor of Cleveland, Michael DiSalle (D) served as mayor of Toledo, and James Rhodes (R) was mayor of Columbus before becoming state auditor and then the longest-serving governor in Ohio history. George Voinovich (R) served in multiple Cuyahoga County offices, then as lieutenant governor, followed by a stint as mayor of Cleveland before he was elected governor of Ohio.

In a change from tradition, members or former members of Congress are now seeking to become governor. Prior to Ted Strickland's successful run for governor in 2006, only Clarence Brown, who won the Republican nomination in 1982 but was defeated in the general election by Richard Celeste, emerged as a candidate from the U.S. house of representatives.[3] Today, the last two governors of Ohio, Strickland and Kasich, served in the U.S. house of representatives as their last elective office before being elected governor; moreover, neither one had run statewide before they were elected governor. These last two Ohio governors also defied the old Ohio political adage "one to meet, twice to win." David Stewart and his coauthors wrote that "every Ohio governor and U.S. Senator elected since 1958 has previously lost at least one statewide race."[4]

Ohio Governor's Office

A recent Ohio budget shows that the Ohio governor's office has 44 employees. This staff includes press spokespersons, legal counsel, policy advisors, schedulers, appointments officials, clerical support, and travel and event planners. Within the governor's office, the chief of staff is usually the person with the most influence, serving as both a gatekeeper for access to the governor and as an agenda setter.

The Roles of the Ohio Governor

The various roles played by Ohio's governor are quite similar to the role played by most governors throughout the nation. These include functioning as the head of state, legislative leader, chief budget official, chief of security and safety, grantor of clemency, party leader, crises manager, and finally, the intergovernmental manager. Each of these roles is discussed below.

Head of State

As the head of state, the governor of Ohio is the top dignitary of the state, receiving notable foreign officials visiting Ohio. As governor, he or she is to appear at official ceremonies and public events. Ohio's governors, especially the current Governor Kasich, enjoy cutting ribbons for new and expanding businesses in the state. Former Governor Robert Taft christened many of the new and remodeled schools constructed as part of the state's response to school funding decisions made by the Ohio supreme court. The governor also speaks for Ohioans on the national stage and is expected to be on the scene in cases of natural and man-made disasters and crises, even if the state can do little about it.

Legislative Leader

The governor has a significant role in setting the legislative agenda for the Ohio general assembly. The Ohio governor will lay out some general legislative policy goals in his annual State of State Address to the Ohio general assembly, which is offered in the beginning of each legislative session. Until Governor Kasich changed the practice, the State of the State Address was always given in the state capital in Columbus. Governor Kasich, however, decided to move the State of the State Address to other parts of Ohio. In 2012, he gave his State of the State Address in Steubenville, which is in the southeast corner of the state. In 2013, Governor Kasich traveled to the opposite corner of the state to give his address in Lima. The governor's 2014 State of the State Address was held in Medina, the home of the outgoing Speaker of the house, William Batchelder.

The Ohio governor can call a special session of the legislature and define the issue that is to be addressed. He or she also has extensive veto power, including what is called the *line item veto*. Kasich vetoed 22 items in the fiscal year (FY) 2014–2015 budget. The headline veto was the legislative restraint on the expansion of Medicaid.

As an informal power, the governor of Ohio can gain access to the state media to present his legislative proposals and will travel around the state presenting his legislative ideas to newspaper editorial boards and hold press conferences to try to influence the Ohio general assembly. The governor has a state plane and the Ohio state highway patrol to get him to his various destinations. Governor Kasich was, for example, able to use this informal power to persuade

kasichforohio.com

Governor Kasich in Lima, Ohio

the legislature to tap the Ohio turnpike tolls for highway projects outside the turnpike. Nevertheless, this power has its limits. Governor Kasich traveled throughout the state making speeches promoting the Medicaid expansion. In the end, however, he was unable to move the Republican legislature to expand Medicaid under the Affordable Care Act.

Youngstown State University

Former Ohio State Senate President Harry Meshel

Usually, the Ohio governor's legislative success, or lack of it, is determined by whether there is divided government in the state. Still, Governor Strickland, a Democrat, was able to achieve a number of his legislative goals in his first two years, despite having to work with Republican majorities in the Ohio house and senate. In this way, Governor Strickland followed the pattern set by Governor Rhodes who, although a Republican, developed a close working relationship with powerful Democrats such as senate President Harry Meshel and Speaker Vern Riffe. Governor Kasich enjoyed a unified government in his first term, yet his initiatives were met with mixed success. One of the problems may be that Governor Kasich appears to prefer announcing his policy proposals before talking to the legislative leaders.

Chief Budget Official

Relative to other states, the budget-making power of the governor of Ohio is "very strong."[5] Every two years, the governor submits his biennial budget four weeks after the general assembly begins (there is an extension to March 15th for newly elected governors). The executive budget becomes the budget document to which the legislature responds. As it is in nearly every state (Vermont being the only exception), Ohio is not allowed to run a formal budget deficit. The amount of proposed spending is therefore related to the Office of Budget and Management's revenue forecasts for the future fiscal years. The legislature develops and passes the budget based on the budget document provided by the executive. Of course, the legislature can and does make changes to the governor's requests. Article II, Section 16 of the Ohio constitution, however, states, "[T]he governor may disapprove any item or items in a bill making an appropriation of money." This is what is known as the *line item veto*. The governor can only make item vetoes to appropriation bills. Therefore, if the Ohio legislature includes substantive provisions of law in appropriation bills, an Ohio court may be called upon to define what constitutes an appropriations *item*. In the past, governors have used the line item to strike complete paragraphs, a sentence, and even single words.[6] Line item vetoes are similar

Ohio Historical Society, James A. Rhodes Collection

James Rhodes, Ohio's longest-serving governor

to regular vetoes (of entire bills) in that they may be overridden by a three-fifths vote of both houses of the general assembly.

Chief of Security and Safety

The Ohio governor has the power to call out the Ohio National Guard to respond to emergencies. Frequently, these are natural disasters such as floods and snowstorms in Ohio. They can, however, also be man-made threats to life and property. In one of the most well-known and tragic events in U.S. history, Governor Rhodes called out the Ohio National Guard to maintain order during the student antiwar protests at Kent State University in 1970. That ended with the death of four people. In January 1978, Governor Rhodes called out the Ohio National Guard to plow snow and rescue stranded motorists in what (at the time) was the worst snowstorm to hit Ohio in sixty-eight years.[7] In the 1980s, Governor Celeste tried to stop the national government from deploying the Ohio National Guard for training exercises in Honduras. The governor lost that battle in federal court.

Grantor of Clemency

The governor of Ohio has the almost-unlimited power of clemency. During his first three years in office, Governor Kasich received 1,031 applications for clemency. He approved 51 of those applications. Clemency can be given in the form of a pardon or a commutation. A pardon is an act that forgives guilt. One of the more notable pardons to occur in Ohio was Governor Rhodes's pardon of flamboyant boxing promoter Don King in 1983. King had been convicted of manslaughter in 1966.

A commutation is different in that it focuses on the punishment rather than the offence. When governors use the commutation power, they reduce the penalty or sentence that is attached to a conviction.[8] Five of those approved for clemency by Governor Kasich involved the commuting of the death penalty.[9] In an additional case, Governor Kasich made history by using his commutation power to postpone the execution of convicted child killer Ron Phillips long enough for Phillips to donate a kidney to a family member.

Party Leader

The Ohio governor is the state leader of his or her party in the state. Governor Kasich, whose endorsement was sought by most of the Republican presidential hopefuls in 2012, did not openly endorse any of them. When the roll call was made at the National Republican Convention, however, he did speak for the Ohio delegation in support of Mitt Romney. Kasich, similar to some governors before him, was at odds with the state chairman of the Ohio Republican Party when he was elected. Kasich and his allies believed that state Chairman Kevin DeWine did not give him the full support of the party in the election of 2010. Kasich and his allies mounted a campaign in the state central committee to oust DeWine. A temporary compromise was reached when elder statesman Bob Bennett was called back into service to lead the party for the failed 2012 Romney campaign in Ohio. A strong Kasich supporter, Matt Borges, was put in as the executive director of the state Republican Party. With the support of Kasich and all of the Ohio Republican Party leaders, Borges replaced Bennett as Republican state party chair in late April 2013.

Ohio Governor Ted Strickland at the 2008 Democratic National Convention

In 2006, Democratic gubernatorial candidate Ted Strickland indicated he wanted Chris Redfern to be the state Democratic chairman. Redfern was elected state democratic chair with little controversy. Redfern, a member of the Ohio house at the time, returned to the house in 2012 and has also stayed on as state democratic chair. He has been a vocal critic of Governor Kasich and the Ohio Republicans.

Crisis Manager

Ohio governors are often confronted with unexpected crises, which come in many forms, and the state's response or lack of it often defines that particular governor. Confronting natural disasters, such as massive snowstorms, floods, or tornadoes, often requires the governor to call out the Ohio National Guard. The governor will also ask the federal government to declare certain impacted areas of the state *disaster areas*. Sometimes governors are also called upon to deal with man-made crisis. In 1985, Governor Celeste was confronted with the unexpected default of the savings and loan industry in Ohio, which led to actual bank closings. Ohio was one of the few states that operated a private insurance fund for savings and loans, and so the banks did not have federal insurance.[10] Governor Voinovich was confronted with inmate riots and the taking of guards as hostages by inmates at the state's Lucasville State Prison.

Intergovernmental Manager

There are numerous federal categorical and block grants that the state manages. The departments under the governor bear the responsibility to administer these grants. In some instances, the state manages the implementation of the federal program. Also, the state is sometimes required to match federal money with state funding. Medicaid is the largest federal grant Ohio receives. The state has limited discretion in defining eligibility and benefits but can seek waivers of federal Medicaid requirements. The Affordable Care Act requires states to provide Medicaid to everyone at 138 percent of the federal poverty level or below. The U.S. Supreme Court famously proclaimed that states are not required to implement that federal legal requirement but have the discretion to do so if they wish. Governor Kasich supported the expansion of Medicaid but was rebuffed by the legislature. Kasich finally got his way by action of the Ohio Controlling Board. Another key part of the Affordable Care Act was the establishment of exchanges by the states. An exchange is basically a marketplace where individuals who do not have health insurance can go to buy health insurance. Depending on their income, individuals will receive some federal subsidy for purchase of the insurance. The federal law does not require the state to establish an exchange, and if a state does not create an exchange, the federal government will establish the exchange for the particular state. The Kasich administration decided not to establish a health insurance exchange and defaulted to the federal government to establish the exchange in Ohio.

The governor also deals with the many local governments within Ohio. An example is the Ohio Department of Transportation (ODOT), which works with Ohio county engineers on road and bridge projects that involve the use of federal funds. Ohio is one of the few states that uses its Jobs and Family Services Agency within each county for the disbursement of various social welfare benefits. The state has numerous own-source grants and federal grants that it disburses to local governments and special districts with some discretion. Governor Kasich, in his first budget, made a very severe cut in Ohio's local government fund, which provided general purposes funds to local governments in the state.

Ohio Executive Officers

There are four other separately elected executive offices in Ohio: the Ohio attorney general, the Ohio secretary of state, the auditor of state of Ohio, and the treasurer of state of Ohio. All of these officials are elected for four-year terms in the midterm election year. They are all term limited to two consecutive four-year terms.

The separately elected administrative officials can become a problem for the governor of Ohio. Attorney General Marc Dann, who was elected on the coattails of Governor Strickland in 2006, became an embarrassment to Strickland because of his hiring of questionable associates and overall frat-boy antics in Columbus. Governor Strickland threatened to have him impeached and thereby forced his resignation. Governor Kasich has found that the Republican state auditor and treasurer, who were elected when he was elected, could be a thorn in his side. The state treasurer, Josh Mandel, elected in the 2010 Ohio Republican landslide, challenged Governor Kasich's FY 2014–2015 budget on a number of key points. First, he publicly opposed the Medicaid expansion that Kasich proposed under the Affordable Care Act. Then, during the same budget cycle, Mandel came out against Kasich's proposed increase of the severance tax for the expected fracking boom in Ohio.

In 2013, state auditor Dave Yost, also a Republican, issued a subpoena for records of the Kasich-created controversial JobsOhio program. Republican leaders in the Ohio general assembly were critical of Yost for his headline-seeking behavior at the expense of the Ohio governor. The Republican state legislature quickly moved to pass a law to shield JobsOhio from Yost's demand to conduct an audit.

Attorney General

The office of attorney general in Ohio was made an elective office by the Ohio constitution of 1851. The attorney general is the chief legal officer for the state, representing all state offices, boards, and commissions. The attorney general's office participates in all civil and criminal cases in which the state has an interest. In recent decades, the attorney general has had to defend Ohio state law and regulations in federal court. During the 2012 general election, for example, Attorney General Mike DeWine was the counsel responsible for defending federal court regulations issued by the Ohio secretary of state on early voting and provisional ballots.

The Ohio attorney general renders legal opinions to public entities, including state agencies and local governments, in the state of Ohio. The attorney general cannot render an opinion to a private entity. A review of recent opinions posted on the attorney general's website will show that the county prosecutor makes the most frequent requests for opinions. The legal weight of the opinion, while persuasive, is neither conclusive nor binding.

Over the years, the attorney general has taken on additional duties. A significant one is the supervision of the Bureau of Criminal Identification and Investigation (BCI), which was created in 1963. This bureau provides local law enforcement and county prosecutor offices with modern analytical methods of investigating crimes. For example, Attorney General DeWine, through the BCI, led a recent independent investigation of an incident in Cleveland during which

60 police vehicles and 115 police officers were involved in a chase that ended with a couple being killed by a storm of police bullets. DeWine's office also took over the prosecution of an alleged rape case by football players in Steubenville, Ohio, in 2012. The attorney general ends up in the middle of these hot political issues because he or she is asked to take a role. In May of 2013, DeWine was quoted as saying, "We're now in 21 active homicide cases. We're in 36 sexual assault cases. In each of these cases, we were asked by the prosecuting attorney to come in and handle the case."[11]

The attorney general can also initiate or join in litigation on behalf of the state before the federal courts. Under DeWine, Ohio joined many other states in challenging the Affordable Care Act (Obamacare). In 2013, DeWine signed a letter to Kathleen Sebelius, then secretary of health and human services, urging that the exemption to the coverage mandate extended to certain nonprofit religious organizations be broadened to include private employers who object to the contraception benefit on religious grounds.[12]

Secretary of State

The secretary of state is the chief elections officer of the state of Ohio. In this capacity, the secretary of state appoints members of the county boards of election after receiving recommendations from the respective county parties. The secretary of state administers election law and reviews statewide initiatives and referendum petitions. In Ohio, the secretary of state also chairs the five-member Ohio ballot board, a committee that must approve ballot language for statewide issues. The secretary of state maintains a record of election-related statistics and is the recipient of the campaign finance reports of statewide candidates, state committees, state political parties, and legislative caucus campaign committees. Political parties prize the secretary of state's office in part because it is one of the three offices included on the state apportionment board that, every ten years, draws the state legislative districts.

The secretary of state also has nonelection-related duties. For example, he or she officially grants authority to companies and individuals to do business in Ohio and keeps records of all the laws passed by the general assembly and all the executive orders issued by the governor.

For many years, the secretary of state's office was seen purely as a nonpolitical administrative agency. It began to change after former Secretary of State Bob Taft moved to the office of governor in 1998 and Republican Kenneth Blackwell was elected to replace him as secretary of state. Blackwell was often accused of using the office to issue rulings that favored his party. After this, secretaries of state from both parties began to introduce legislation and issue administrative rules that were seen by the opposing political party as being motivated to impact the outcome of presidential elections.

During the 2012 presidential election, the Republican secretary of state, Jon Husted, issued rules that were frequently contested by Democrats. Husted, for example, tried to put a limit on early voting in the three days preceding the general elections. The Obama campaign challenged this ruling in federal court, and Husted was ordered to reverse his decision. This remains a contentious issue. In 2014, Husted issued an order directed at establishing uniform hours for early voting the weekend before the general election. That directive did not include hours for early voting on the Sunday before Election Day. In 2008, that was a day when African American churches in Ohio had mobilized to vote. Once again, the same federal judge (who Republicans pointed out had been appointed to the bench by a Democratic president, Bill Clinton) ordered Husted to restore early in-person voting on the three days before Election Day.[13]

Finally, the secretary of state is sometimes drawn into local political disputes if a close election result leads to a recount of votes. County boards of election, which are composed of two Democrats and two Republicans, are often unable to reach a final decision on disputed ballots. In these cases, the secretary of state provides the tie-breaking vote.

Auditor

Every two years, the Ohio auditor conducts postaudits of state agencies and units of local governments. This responsibility is termed *legal-fiscal audits* and the audits determine the legality and propriety of expenditures. This is in contrast to *performance audits*, which address issues such as efficiency. The state auditor will conduct performance audits if there is a request. Occasionally, there is a postaudit letter to a department or political subdivision issued by the auditor that addresses management issues. In recent decades, the audit function is contracted out to accounting firms, who perform the audits. If the auditor discovers an error on the financial activities of a state agency or a local government, the resulting report will make recommendations for the recovery of the funds. Recommendations will also be made to prevent a reoccurrence of this error. The auditor will also provide technical assistance to local governments.

The state auditor in Ohio has the legal power to restrict the financial authority of local governments and school districts if they do not meet certain fiscal measures. For example, if there is a deficit in the general fund or any other fund that exceeds one-twelfth of the total general budget, then the local government is placed on fiscal watch. If the deficit exceeds one-sixth of the general fund budget, then the local government goes into fiscal emergency and a commission is created to provide oversight of that government. These commissions are given broad control over the finances of the affected local government. They must approve most financial transactions and are in charge of developing a recovery plan.

For school districts, the auditor works jointly with the Ohio Department of Education to make fiscal watch and fiscal emergency designations. The triggers are slightly different from those in place for local governments. A fiscal emergency is declared if a forecasted operating deficit for the current FY exceeds 15 percent of the school district's general fund revenue for the preceding FY. If a fiscal emergency is declared, the oversight commission formed "can assume any powers of the school board it considers necessary."[14]

Recently, the auditor conducted a review of reported student attendance data. This was initiated, in part, by the No Child Left Behind (NCLB) Act of 2001. Under NCLB, each school's "report card" (evaluation) specifies its performance as compared to other schools in the state in certain subjects. The students included in the scoring can impact the school's performance on the report. If low-performing students are excluded from the overall number, then performance is seemingly improved. The auditor capturing this cheating serves as an example of the evolving obligations of state agencies that are often increased by the demands of federal policies.

In early 2013, it was reported that thirty-five schools in five districts had manipulated student data. Schools in Toledo and Columbus had engaged in this fraud by temporarily withdrawing students and them reenrolling those students so their test scores and attendance would not be counted. The individual who masterminded this scheme in the Columbus school system resigned. The state auditor identified another 100 schools that might have also "scrubbed" their student data. There are more than 3,200 traditional public schools in the state.[15]

The auditor's office in Ohio was once a bastion of political patronage. This has changed since term limits were imposed on the auditor (and all other statewide constitutional officers) through an initiative on the 1992 ballot. The auditor's position is still considered a political party prize, however, because, similar to the secretary of state, the auditor sits on the state apportionment board. Although the office of auditor of Ohio has occasionally served as a stepping stone to a higher office, it receives very little public attention, since it is primarily an administrative and not a policy-making office.

Treasurer

The Ohio treasurer is responsible for investing the state's funds for safekeeping and for disbursing warrants (checks) in payment for state obligations. The treasurer serves on the Ohio State Board of Deposit, which invests the state monies in state banks and savings and loan associations throughout the state. The treasurer is also a member of the Sinking Fund Commission, which is responsible for administering the sale of state bonds and the redemption of bonded debt.

This office, like the auditor's office, is an administrative and not a policy-making office; consequently, it has little public visibility. The current Ohio Treasurer Mandel tried to generate publicity by posting Ohio public employees' salaries on the department's website. Although he earned the ire of state employees, he did receive considerable press for this action. Treasurer Mandel tried to use his post as a stepping stone to the U.S. senate in 2012. Although he ran a hard campaign, he was, in the end, decisively defeated by the incumbent Democratic senator, Sherrod Brown.

The Governor's Cabinet

Every Ohio governor has a formal cabinet consisting of individuals who, by virtue of their position, run an important department under the executive branch. Governor Kasich has a cabinet of twenty-six members. A list of all of the cabinet departments is provided in Table 4.1.

TABLE 4.1 Cabinet Departments

CABINET DEPARTMENTS	
Adjutant General	Administrative Services
Aging	Agriculture
Alcohol and Drug Addiction Services	(Office of) Budget and Management
Commerce	Development Services Agency
Developmental Disabilities	Environmental Protection Agency
Health	Transformation Health
Insurance	Jobs and Family Services
Medicaid	Mental Health
Natural Resources	Public Safety
Public Utilities Commission	Regents
Rehabilitation and Correction	Taxation
Transportation	Veterans Services
Bureau of Workers' Compensation	Youth Services

Data source: "Administration: Cabinet," John R. Kasich, Governor of Ohio, accessed October 11, 2014, http://www.governor.ohio.gov/Administration/Cabinet.aspx

It has become common in Ohio government for the lieutenant governor to take leadership of a cabinet department. Mary Taylor, the current lieutenant governor, also serves as Ohio's insurance commissioner. The duties of the insurance commissioner became more complex under Taylor. She had to address some of the challenges presented by the Affordable Care Act. As already discussed, Ohio declined to create a state exchange and deferred to the federal government; however, other issues arose when President Obama extended the length of time someone could retain their nonqualifying individual insurance, since those polices are state regulated.

Some of the Ohio cabinet departments, such as Aging and Veterans Services, provide services to defined constituencies. Others are regulatory, such as insurance and the Ohio Environmental Protection Agency. Some departments become more significant because of demands placed on them. The Ohio Department of Natural Resources has taken on a demanding and controversial role, since it is the agency that issues drilling permits for high-volume horizontal hydraulic fracturing (fracking) to reach natural gas deposits found in eastern Ohio, which is expected to be a booming industry in Ohio (see Box 4.1).

BOX 4.1: The Fracking Boom in Ohio

The headline for a *CNN Money* piece published late in 2011 read, "Ohio set to see oil boom thanks to fracking."[1] Ohio, the birthplace of John D. Rockefeller's Standard Oil, was once a national economic powerhouse. In recent decades, however, that state has suffered from significant deindustrialization. This ongoing problem was exacerbated by the Great Recession, which hit the state hard beginning in the fall of 2008. Therefore, news of an impending windfall of jobs and money was very welcome in the Buckeye state. Thomas Stewart of the Ohio Oil and Gas Association concluded that "[it was] one of the most significant economic events to occur in Ohio in decades."[2] Stewart projected that over 200,000 new jobs would eventually come to Ohio and that Ohio would become sixth in the nation in oil production. Yet, for some environmentalists, fracking—more accurately known as *unconventional* or *shale gas drilling*—is fraught with significant environmental risks. There is also growing skepticism about the actual size of the so-called fracking boom for Ohio.

The fracking process is one during which companies create cracks in shale rock to extract gas, oil, and other substances. The process begins with a well drilled about 6,000 to 8,000 feet vertically and then drilled horizontally between 4,000 and 8,000 feet into the rock layer containing natural gas. Millions (typically 5 million) of gallons of water, mixed with sand and other chemical additives, are injected into the well. This pressurized fluid fractures the shale and opens cracks so the gas flows into the well. The contaminated fluid must then be stored in underground wells called *injection wells*.

Fracking is exempt from significant federal regulation. Barbara Warner and Jennifer Shapiro have written on this issue, observing that "fracking is given many special exemptions from federal law that are not granted most other heavy industries."[3] These authors point out that Congress exempted oil and gas waste from regulation of hazardous waste under the Resource Conservation and Recovery Act (RCRA) of 1976. Fracking is also exempted from disclosure requirements under the federal Emergency Planning and Community Right to Know Act. This act requires companies to submit annual Toxic Chemical Release Forms that report their use of toxic chemicals to the U.S. Environmental Protection Agency (EPA). Fracking companies maintain that use of some chemicals is proprietary. This issue of what chemicals are used is a concern to environmental groups that are focused on fracking. Neither the federal Clean Water Act (CWA) that deals with disposal issues nor the Hazardous Materials Transportation Act (HMTA) that covers transportation regulate these key parts of the fracking industry. Notably, fracking waste is exempt from the Safe Drinking Water Act's (SDWA) underground injection well requirements. The 2005 Energy Policy Act affirmed it was the state, not the federal government, that had jurisdiction over the oil and gas industry.[4]

In 2004, the Ohio general assembly passed House Bill 278, which empowered a single state agency, the Ohio Department of Natural Resources (ODNR), to regulate oil and gas fracking in the state. Drilling permits are issued through the division of Oil and Gas Resources Management. The division chief has delegated authority to issue permits and to locate and space oil and gas wells within the state. The department is funded partially by fees it collects. This leaves local governments in Ohio with no say in regulating this industry.[5]

Fracking gained national attention with the release of the documentary film, *Gasland*. *Gasland*, produced by amateur documentarian Josh Fox, was highly critical of the fracking industry, which the industry said was inaccurate. The classic scene in the film is fire coming out of the faucet in the kitchen sink, implying that the drinking water had been contaminated. Supporters of fracking industry take issue with many of the claims made in the documentary, pointing out, for example, that inflammable water may have many possible causes.[6]

Another issue of public concern about fracking involves not the process itself but the disposal of liquid waste. As pointed out above, injection wells are not subject to significant federal regulation and the state is the major regulator permitting agency. There have been allegations of earthquakes caused by the injection wells in Arkansas, New Mexico, Ohio, Oklahoma, and Texas. There were a series of earthquakes in Youngstown, Ohio, near an injection well. Of particular concern was an earthquake that occurred in Youngstown on New Year's Eve in 2012 that registered a 4.0 magnitude. As a result of that event, the ODNR had to shut down five wells within a

(Continued)

(Continued)

seven-mile radius of the earthquake and froze the application process for new injection wells. According to a Columbia University seismic expert, the New Year's Eve earthquake was most likely caused by fluid from an injection well leaking into a fault line.[7] New well rules were enacted and seismic tests can now be ordered by ODNR officials before new wells are approved. In late 2012, new permits for injection wells began to be approved. The *Plain Dealer* reported that Portage County could have as many as 25 injection wells, "which would make it the leading disposal area for fracking waste in the state."[8] State Representative Kathleen Clyde, a house Democrat who represents most of Portage County, said the new wave of injection wells in her area was a concern and asked why Ohio was becoming the "bargain basement state" for getting rid of "toxic waste."[9]

On the Republican side, Governor Kasich has also expressed concern about the out-of-state liquid waste produced by fracking coming to Ohio, noting, "When people are using our things, and they could disrupt our ability to have progress here, we have to be concerned about it." Kasich went on to say that his administration "[was] thinking about what [they could] do and not violate the interstate commerce clause."[10]

Finally, beyond the environmental concerns raised by fracking, there are growing doubts about the magnitude of the economic boom from fracking predicted earlier. It appears, however, that it is simply too early to tell. As Dr. Jeffrey Dick of the Department of Geological and Environmental Sciences at Youngstown State University put it, "The early expectations were unrealistic. People expected the shale to be developed much quicker than realistically possible."[11]

Notes

1. Steve Hargreaves, "Ohio Set to See Oil Boom Thanks to Fracking," *CNN Money*, December 20, 2011, accessed October 12, 2014, http://money.cnn.com/2011/12/20/news/economy/ohio_oil/.
2. Ibid.
3. Barbara Warner and Jennifer Shapiro, "Fractured, Fragmented Federalism: A Study in Fracking Regulatory Policy," *Publius: The Journal of Federalism Advance Access* (April 18, 2013): 5.
4. Ibid, 7.
5. "Community Bill of Rights Ensures Democratic Local Control," *Valley Voice* (Spring 2013): 1, accessed October 13, 2014, http://www.mvorganizing.org/images/Spring%20VV%202013.pdf
6. Michael Economides, "Slurring Natural Gas with Flaming Faucets and Other Propaganda," *Forbes*, April 22, 2010, accessed October 13, 2014,

http://www.forbes.com/sites/greatspeculations/2010/04/22/slurring-natural-gas-with-flaming-faucets-and-other-propaganda/

7. Aaron Marshall, "New Wave of Injection Wells on the Way in Ohio for Fracking Waste," *Plain Dealer,* November 24, 2012.
8. Ibid.
9. Ibid.
10. Mark Niquette, "Ohio Tries to Escape Fate as a Dumping Ground for Fracking Fluid," *Bloomberg News,* January 31, 2012, accessed October 13, 2014, http://www.bloomberg.com/news/2012-02-01/ohio-tries-to-escape-fate-as-a-dumping-ground-for-fracking-fluid.html.
11. Burton Speakman, "Economics, Technology Drive Utica Shale Decisions," *The Vindicator,* June 15, 2013, accessed October 13, 2014, http://www.vindy.com/news/2013/jun/15/technology-costs-factor-into-utica-decis/?fracking

Governor Kasich has focused on Medicaid and designated it as a separate cabinet department. Medicaid consumes a large part of Ohio's budget, and the new cabinet department is expected to look for ways to contain the budget growth in Medicaid and address a number of issues that are a result of the federal Affordability Care Act.

Selected Cabinet Departments

Economic Development

Ohio's governors take a strong interest in economic development because it is one of the measures of success of their term in office as well as a source of positive earned media. The Department of Development in Ohio has long been the instrument of state government to attract and retain jobs. Governor Kasich separated this agency into two separate entities. Effective September 28, 2012, the name of the existing agency was formally changed from the Department of Development to the Ohio Development Services Agency (ODSA). The functions of ODSA are now purely administrative. The tools used by the state of Ohio for economic development were relocated to a new entity created by the legislature at the behest of Governor Kasich, called JobsOhio.

JobsOhio controls Ohio's various incentives to attract business investment to the state and create jobs. JobsOhio offers low-interest loans, tax credits, and venture capital.[16] JobsOhio has been termed *privatization* by both its detractors and its supporters, but it is more accurately termed a "semi-private agency."[17] The funding stream for this new entity included $1 million appropriated by the legislature. In addition, the legislature gave the new agency permission to enter into a complex lease of the state's wholesale liquor profits. The lease was purchased with the proceeds of $1.5 billion in bonds. An appointed board governs this not-for-profit economic development agency.

One common criticism of this reorganization effort is that the JobsOhio legislation creates a special nonprofit public-private corporation that lacks transparency yet is able to invest public funds and grant tax benefits to selected private business ventures. Governor Kasich maintains that this new form of nonprofit nongovernmental economic development will be more effective because it will not be hindered by government regulations and will work at the "speed of business."[18] Although Kasich received support from the Republican-dominated general assembly, Governor Kasich was frustrated by Democratic legislators and liberal policy groups, such as ProgressOhio, who challenged the constitutionality of JobsOhio in the Ohio supreme court. Brian Rothenberg, executive director of ProgressOhio, said "The money came from a source that is public . . . and just because the legislature plays games with the law, legislatures can't supersede the Ohio Constitution."[19] The Ohio supreme court ruled in June of 2014 that the parties did not have standing to sue.

Auditor Yost, a Republican, sought to audit the books of JobsOhio but was blocked by the state legislature. The argument made by the Kasich administration was that for JobsOhio to be effective, it should be free of the constraints of the state's slow-moving bureaucracy.

There is a certain irony in the fact that while the apparent intent in creating JobsOhio was to shield economic development deals between private businesses and the state from public scrutiny, its creation led to greater scrutiny. The stir created by the demand for records by the state auditor and the response of further protection for JobsOhio by the Republican-dominated legislature has led to greater scrutiny than if state economic development had remained simply part of the state bureaucracy. The Ohio Democrats, seeking traction for the 2014 state elections, used JobsOhio as one of their talking points, trying to convince voters that something was being hidden that, when revealed, would bring down the Kasich government.

Under the JobsOhio program, the state awarded 181 "Job Creation" tax breaks, worth a record-breaking $132 million in 2011. The tax breaks were granted to companies threatening to leave the state but were also used to attract new industry to the state. Since the tax break is awarded over time, not all of that revenue is lost in the first year.

JobsOhio works with six regional economic districts around the state. These regional districts are comprised of county governments and chambers of commerce organizations. They have been instructed to deemphasize retention tax credits and now are to attract companies by creating a broader, friendlier business climate and reinforcing the idea that Ohio is an attractive place to do business.

In December 2012, the *New York Times* ran a three-part series that reported that state and local governments nationwide gave out $80 billion in incentives annually to businesses. It is not clear whether Governor Kasich was influenced by the story, but after that series ran, he said, "We've kind of discontinued that practice here in the state."[20] He went on to say that Ohio is not giving away the store and getting into bidding wars with other states. This last issue has long been a controversial issue in the study of state government. States have tried to outbid each other to attract new investments, especially large investments that promise many well-paying jobs. Some critics maintain that the corporations benefit more than the taxpayers.

The use of financial incentives to attract and retain industries is not only a controversial issue because the state is often foregoing revenue or giving out state revenue, it is a controversial practice because the expectations of the number of jobs resulting from the deal are often not met. A report from Attorney General DeWine showed that of the 255 economic development contracts concluded in 2011, 93 of the beneficiaries failed to meet their obligations. The recipients received $144 worth of benefits (either loans, tax breaks, or grants) in exchange for employee training or hiring or maintaining certain wage levels.[21] The awards in the report were approved between 2006 and 2008 and ended in 2011. None of these deals, therefore, were done under the Kasich administration. These were very difficult years for the Ohio economy, but there is growing scrutiny and questions about the value of using state revenue to outbid other states for economic development projects that often do not meet expectations.

Office of Budget and Management

Another key cabinet member and agency for the governor of Ohio is the Office of Budget and Management (OBM). Governor John Gilligan had created the OBM in 1973. Ten years later, Rhodes, the longest-serving governor in Ohio history, reportedly told his successor, Celeste, that the most important appointment he would make was the director of Ohio's OBM. One reason for the importance of Ohio's OBM is that the budget must end in balance at the end of the FY, which in Ohio is June 30th. OBM does the executive's revenue forecasts. If it appears that the budget will not be balanced at the end of each FY, then the budget will have to be cut by the executive or he or she will have to seek additional revenues. Neither one of these are attractive options to ambitious politicians. The OBM prepares and presents the various executive budget proposals to the legislature. The Ohio budget process will be discussed in Chapter 7.

Medicaid

Medicaid was passed as a federal program in 1965 under President Lyndon Johnson. Medicaid is a joint federal-state program. The states can choose to participate in the Medicaid program, and all fifty states now participate. Medicaid has become the largest federal grant to the state of Ohio, and Ohio is obligated to provide matching funds. Ohio, like all states, has some flexibility in determining program eligibility and benefits. Medicaid provides health benefits to certain defined population groups, including the aged, the blind, the disabled, and families with children who meet certain income requirement. Eligibility is frequently stated as a certain percentage of the federal poverty level (for example, uninsured children in families with incomes up to the federal poverty level or pregnant women at 200 percent of the federal poverty level). Many aged Ohioans who are in nursing homes are on Medicaid. That program has become the de facto nursing home insurer in Ohio and the United States. According to the Kaiser Institute, long-term care accounted for 40 percent of Ohio's Medicaid budget in FY 2010–2011.

Medicaid has risen to such importance in Ohio's budget that Governor Kasich proposed that it became a freestanding Ohio cabinet-level department agency. The Medicaid department was split from the Ohio Jobs and Family Services Agency, which manages other social welfare programs. To prepare for the transition toward a stand-alone Ohio state Medicaid cabinet department, the governor, in his first weeks in office, issued an executive order that created an Office of Health Transformation. The Ohio Department of Medicaid was finally established in July of 2013.

The Kasich administration stated at the time that Medicaid accounted for 30 percent of the state budget. The total cost of Medicaid in 2012 was $18.8 billon, which included $6.4 billion in state funds. OBM Director Tim Keen testified, "Medicaid currently provides health care services to over 2.3 million Ohioans per month at a projected cost of $19.768 billion."[22] The Kasich administration argued that even if nothing was done about changing Medicaid eligibility, the Affordable Care Act and the requirement of the individual mandate would generate an additional enrolled population of 230,000 people who would "come out of the woodwork" and become enrolled in Medicaid by June 2015.[23] This became known as the *woodwork effect.*

As already discussed, the Affordable Care Act or Obamacare required the states to provide Medicaid not only to specific populations but also to everyone who was at or below 138 percent of the federal poverty level. To relieve the burden on the states, the federal government would provide all of the funds in the initial years of the new program. The federal reimbursement for the first three years will be at 100 percent and then will decrease to 90 percent by 2020. In 2012, the U.S. Supreme

Court in the case ruled that the federal government could not require the state to provide this additional Medicaid coverage and that the state could choose not to participate.[24]

In his second biennium budget in 2013, Governor Kasich proposed adopting Medicaid expansion. Governor Kasich's decision to expand Medicaid eligibility to 138 percent of the federal poverty level changes eligibility guidelines in such a way that that some individuals eligible for Medicaid under current guidelines will no longer be eligible and will likely move to the federal health care exchange. This will lead to a state-projected savings on Medicaid spending of $22.9 million in FY 2014 and $68.2 million in FY 2015.[25]

Transportation

The ODOT is a key cabinet department. It awards prized non-bid contracts to engineering firms and takes bids for major construction projects. Like Medicaid, transportation funding is a complex web of federal and state monies and regulations. Although the Ohio transportation system includes highways, railroads, mass transit, aviation, and water, Ohio concentrates most of its attention and funding on highway transportation. When Governor Kasich first took office, he turned back federal stimulus money provided to Ohio for development of passenger rail, partly because of unknown demand and future costs. The transportation bill, though a separate law, is taken up at the same time as the general operating budget bill. For FY 2014–2015, it was a total of $7.6 billion.

The federal government has not raised its 18.4 cents gasoline tax in nearly twenty years. The Ohio general assembly has no interest in raising its gasoline tax of 28 cents, which it shares with county governments. With decaying transportation infrastructure, fewer dollars from the gasoline tax due to a stagnant economy, and more fuel-efficient vehicles, states such as Ohio are looking for alternative revenues, such as tolls, to meet growing infrastructure demands. Governor Kasich, for example, has proposed using tolls to finance a bridge project over the Ohio River in Cincinnati. Ohio has not used tolls to finance bridges since the 1930s. *Governing Magazine* reported that 8.3 percent of Ohio's bridges are structurally deficient. That is below the national average.[26]

One of the most contentious transportation budget issues raised by the Kasich administration in recent years has been over the future of the Ohio Turnpike, a toll road that services the northern part of the state. Some states, such as Indiana, have recently leased their turnpike to private investors, and Governor Kasich considered but eventually rejected such a move early in his term as governor. Instead, the governor proposed to allow the Ohio turnpike to issue bonds against its future toll revenues for non-turnpike transportation projects in northern Ohio. That required a change in legislation, which eventually passed the general assembly. The name of the Ohio Turnpike Commission was changed to the Ohio Turnpike and Infrastructure Commission. After the law was passed, the Turnpike and Infrastructure Commission announced it would raise tolls by 30 percent over the next ten years.

Ohio Department of Rehabilitation and Correction

The state of Ohio incarcerates those convicted of felonies who are subsequently sentenced to a term in state prison. This is a financial strain on the state budget and is an unpredictable expense. To reduce cost and generate revenue, Governor Kasich sold a number of prisons to private operators in the FY 2012–2013 budget period, including the controversial Lucasville prison. On October 29, 2012, the Ohio Department of Rehabilitation and Correction (ODRC) reported that there were 45,931 male prisoners in Ohio state prisons and 3,850 female prisoners, for a total of 49,781 inmates.

Ohio maintains the death penalty and the ODRC carries out that penalty using lethal injection. In December 2012, there were 144 death row inmates in Ohio prisons.

Selected Boards and Commissions

State boards and commissions are another part of the executive branch of Ohio government. They are created by statute and are governed by boards whose members are appointed for a term. Usually, although not always, board members are appointed by the governor, and the Ohio senate must confirm the appointments. Some board members receive financial compensation, but most receive only reimbursement for expenses. The boards and commissions discussed below are some of the more significant ones in the state of Ohio. They also serve as apt examples of the variety of executive responsibilities that boards and commissions exercise in Ohio.

Public Utilities Commission

The Public Utilities Commission of Ohio (PUCO) has wide regulatory authority over utility services in Ohio. The PUCO is governed by a five-person commission appointed by the governor and is subject to senate confirmation. One seat is available each year. The governor's selection is limited to the list provided to his office from the 12-member PUCO Nominating Council. PUCO members are paid a salary, which in 2012 was between $73,715 and $157,955.

The mission of the PUCO is to "[regulate] utilities rates and terms of service for monopoly and non-competitive services."[27] It regulates rates and services of electric, gas, telephone, water, and sewer. The PUCO does not have authority over publicly owned utilities. The PUCO is designed to protect Ohio customer from being gouged by private, for-profit, monopolistic providers of utilities. Utilities seeking to raise their rates or change services have to first plead their case to the PUCO board. There has been some evolution of the role of the PUCO since competition has been introduced in some utility services, such as natural gas. Now, the consumer can now select from a variety of natural gas providers, who solicit customers and offer different prices.

A controversial law freezing renewable and energy efficiency (EE) requirements for two years was passed in June 2014. This weakened an earlier law requiring utilities to sell 12.5 percent of their electricity from renewable sources and reduce their usage 22 percent by 2025 and made Ohio the first state to roll back renewable and EE standards that many states enacted in the last decade.[28] The PUCO's role in this controversy is only administrative. The PUCO is in charge of certifying the renewable projects and approves the EE projects and counts them toward the EE benchmarks established by the earlier law.[29]

Commercial transportation companies in Ohio are public utilities under the jurisdiction of the PUCO. The PUCO registers motor carriers and ensures that they adhere to state and federal safety standards.

Ethics Commission

The Ohio Ethics Law was passed in 1973 and went into effect in 1974. The law established the Ohio Ethics Commission, a six-member bipartisan board appointed by the governor. It created ethical standards for public officials in Ohio and requires annual financial disclosure from many Ohio public officials and employees under its jurisdiction. One of the goals of the financial disclosure requirement is to ascertain whether there are any conflicts of interest for those holding public office. The Ethics Commission seeks to determine whether a public official has a possible personal gain from a public contract the official has influence in awarding. Public officials and public employees are not to misuse their position to benefit themselves. The commission has jurisdiction over Ohio's executive branch and all public officials and employees at the state and local levels of government, except legislators, judges, and their staff, who must report similar information to different entities.

The commission issues numerous advisory opinions to public officials about potential violations of the ethics laws. These opinions have taken on the role of serving as precedents for future opinions on similar topics. The purpose of the opinion is to give guidance before the person under its jurisdiction takes action. The commission states, any person who receives a written advisory opinion from the commission can "reasonably rely" on the opinion and shall be immune from criminal prosecution, civil suits, and removal from his or her office or position based on the facts and circumstances covered by the opinion.[30] Evidence of ethics violations collected by the commission is turned over the respective county prosecutor.

The executive branch is also subject to the Office of Inspector General. This office was permanently created in 1990. The office investigates fraud, abuse, and corruption within the executive branch. Its authority is limited to the governor's staff, state agencies, departments, boards, and commission appointed, controlled, directed, or subject to the authority of the governor. Complaints are investigated and remedial actions are recommended to the specific agency. If appropriate, a report of an investigation may be forwarded to the prosecutor. In 2010, the office received 456 complaints and closed 78 investigations.

State Board of Education

The State Board of Education has 11 members elected from individual districts and eight members appointed by the governor with the advice and consent of the senate. The board selects the Superintendent of Public Instruction. The membership of this board has long been an issue for Ohio governors. Governors argue that, since the general public holds the governor responsible for the quality of public education in the state, the governor ought to be empowered to appoint the members of the State Board of Education. Governor Voinovich in particular fought for greater control of the board but, in the end, had to settle with a compromise of a smaller board and appointing authority over a minority of the membership.

Board of Regents

The Ohio Board of Regents was established under Governor Rhodes in 1963 to govern postsecondary education in Ohio. The Board of Regents has nine members, with one member appointed every year. Its task is to advocate for and manage state funds for public colleges. Prior to its establishment, each individual institution sought its appropriations independently. Since it was created, public higher education has sought a unified operating and capital budget. The Board of Regents acted independently and selected their own chancellor. Under Governor Strickland, however, a change was made, and the chancellor became an appointee of the governor. The chancellor of education in Ohio is now also a member of the governor's cabinet. The regents themselves have become much less influential. The chancellor, who for decades was usually an academician, has recently been selected from among the ranks of former public officials.

State University Boards

Ohio has 13 universities, one free-standing medical school, and numerous community colleges. They are all governed by boards of trustees appointed by the governor and subject to senate confirmation. There are no statutory requirements for appointment to a board of trustees. These higher education institutions are quasi-autonomous. The board of the Ohio State University put then-President Gordon Gee on notice because of the revelation of his jokes about Catholics not inviting Notre Dame into the Big Ten. Gee then resigned. The state colleges in Ohio charge different tuition and fees, although in recent years, the state has capped tuition increases at a certain percentage. The state provides limited funding to these institutions based on a complex formula that emphasizes course completion and graduation rates. There are nonvoting student members appointed by the governor to these respective boards. There is legislation introduced regularly to give the student members of Ohio college boards full voting rights, but those bills have not yet been enacted.

Casino Control Commission

The Ohio Casino Control Commission was established after the constitutional amendment initiative on gambling passed in November of 2009. The adopted constitutional language listed the four cites, and the exact sites, of the new legalized casinos. The amendment was unusually specific, listing the individual tax parcels where the casinos would be built. In addition to designating the locations for the gaming facilities, the amendment stated that the tax on the casinos would be 33 percent of the gross revenue and prohibited state and local governments from levying other casino gaming-related taxes or fees. Because they wrote the constitutional language that was approved by Ohio voters, the gaming interests, not the state legislature, defined the terms and conditions of legalized gambling in Ohio.

The constitutional language specifies that 3 percent of the tax revenue from the gross revenue of the casinos will go to the Casino Control Commission.

Ohio Casino Control Commission

Former Ohio House Speaker Jo Ann Davidson, chair of the Ohio Casino Control Commission

The seven members are appointed by the governor, serve four-year terms, and are paid $60,000 dollars a year. This was changed to $30,000 in the 2014 mid-biennium budget review (MBR). The commissioners are required to have a specific background, such as law or law enforcement. One member must be a certified public accountant. No member of the commission can be affiliated with an Ohio casino operator or facility and not more than four members can be of the same political party.

The commission has no authority to issue additional casino licenses. Its function is to regulate these four newly created casinos. The Ohio Department of Taxation collects the tax from the casinos, although the state of Ohio receives very little of this tax revenue; instead, it is dedicated to county and city governments and a county student fund (based on population). Five percent of the tax revenues generated is returned to the host cities of the four casinos.

The Casino Control Commission has exercised its regulatory authority over these new casinos. For example, it fined the Horseshoe casino in Cleveland $150,000 for using computer software without approval of the regulators. The software allowed gamblers to download credits from their accounts to use for free play on slot machines. It was later approved. In April 2013, the commission fined the same casino $150,000 for use of unapproved dice, mishandling keys, failing to post a gambling problem hotline, encouraging cocktail servers to enter a restricted area between table games, and improperly storing and shipping slot machines.

Professional Licensing and Examination Boards

There are dozens of boards in Ohio created by statute that determine admission standards and qualifications issued by the state and that are required to hold a license and practice certain professions in the state. The only compensation for those serving on the above-mentioned boards, unless otherwise specified, is for expenses. Through these professional licensing commissions, the state of Ohio grants the professional associations the state authority to regulate themselves. Listed below are examples of some of these boards.

Board of Bar Examiners

There are eighteen members on the Board of Bar Examiners who are appointed by the supreme court of Ohio. They serve a five-year term and can have no relationship with any school or university that has an affiliated law school. They must be members of the Ohio Bar in good standing.

Board of Embalmers and Funeral Directors

The governor appoints the seven-member Board of Embalmers and Funeral Directors. Five of the those members must be licensed embalmers and practicing funeral directors with a minimum of ten consecutive years of experience immediately preceding appointment. One of them must have experience operating a crematory. Of the two public members, one must be at least sixty years old.

Dental Board

The State Dental Board has thirteen members, all of whom are appointed by the governor for a four-year term with the advice and consent of the senate. Nine of the members must be dental school graduates and have practiced dentistry in Ohio for the preceding five years. An additional three members are graduates of dental hygiene schools who are U.S. citizens and have had a dental hygiene practice for the past five years. There is one representative who is not associated in any way with the practice of dentistry. When making appointments to this board, governors must take geographical representation into account.[31] Members are limited to two terms.

Influence of Professional Associations

The State Dental Board is a good example of the influence of the professional associations in these groups. Under Ohio law, the "Ohio Dental Association and the Ohio Dental Hygienists Association, Inc. may each submit 5 names for each dentist or dental hygienists appointment."[32] John Gargan, in discussing the numerous boards and commissions, noted that "Interest group leaders recognize that autonomous board or commission status can carry with it a separate funding line in the state budget and protection for their policy concerns from switches in partisan control of the governor's office or legislature."[33] Gargan seemed troubled by the long list of professional boards and commissions in Ohio when he wrote, "The growth and influence of the professions present a dilemma of sorts to state officials. The potential for monopolistic control of their fields by professionals raises serious concerns of protection of the public interest."[34] These professional associations engage in political activity to gain control of their regulatory boards.

There is occasional conflict between the professions because the scope of their authority is defined by state statute. In the 2013 budget, conflict arose between chiropractors and the Ohio State Medical Association. The issue was what type of medical professional would be allowed to place student athletes with head injuries back in the game. Chiropractors were able to gain that authority in the house version of the budget. Tim Miglione, senior director of the Ohio State Medical Association, in an effort to have it taken out of the senate version, said, "I think that when we're talking about head injuries to children, a physician's training and scope of expertise is broader and more comprehensive than a chiropractor."[35] The letter Miglione sent was signed by officials from the Ohio Chapter of the American Academy of Pediatrics, Ohio Children's Hospital Association, Ohio Athletic Trainers Association, Ohio Hospital Association, and the Ohio Osteopathic Association. Kreg Huffer, a chiropractor and spokesman for the Chiropractic Association testified in favor of the language. The amendment cleared the mid-June conference committee and was part of the final budget bill passed by both houses. The Chiropractic Association lost out at the end to the Ohio State Medical Association because Governor Kasich eliminated the language with the use of his line item veto. The Ohio Chiropractic Association was not deterred and was able to get a similar provision on the 2014 MBR.

Sunset Review Committee

A number of Ohio's boards and commissions and other parts of state government to which members are elected or appointed are subject to review by the Sunset Review Committee. The committee is made up of legislators of both houses appointed by leadership. Ohio's Sunset Review Law provides that if the general assembly does not renew or transfer a state agency within an established time frame, the agency expires. A Republican house member who served on the committee, Cheryl Grossman, said that many times, the function of the agency is changed as a result of the sunset review.[36] The committee's recommendations take the form of a bill. Since its inception, it has operated on five-year cycles. Numerous boards and commissions have been abolished by this procedure. Many state agencies are exempt from sunset review. The sunset legislation is not permanent and must be renewed to continue.

Conclusion

The executive branch in Ohio, as in most states, is fragmented, consisting of numerous separately elected offices and appointed boards and commissions. The governor's role in the executive branch and in Ohio government is significant and multifaceted. While Ohio governors are powerful and influential, the demands on them are enormous. Within their four to eight years in office, governors are expected to manage the state, grow the state's economy, and improve both the funding and the quality of the public education system.

Notes

1. Thad L. Beyle, "Being Governor," in *The State of the States,* ed. Carl Van Horn (Washington DC: Congressional Quarterly Press, 1993), 79–114.
2. John J. Gargan, "The Ohio Executive Branch" in *Ohio Politics,* eds. Alexander Lamis and Brian Usher, 2nd ed. (Kent: Kent State University Press, 2007), 399–401.
3. Ibid.
4. David E. Sturrock, Michael Margolis, John C. Green, and Dick Kimmins, "Ohio Elections and Politics in the 1990s," in *Ohio Politics,* eds. Alexander Lamis and Brian Usher, 2nd ed. (Kent: Kent State University Press, 2007), 488.
5. Ibid.
6. Richard Sheridan, *Follow the Money* (Cleveland: Federation of Community Planning, Cleveland, Ohio, 2000), 11.
7. Lee Leonard, " Rhode's Second Eight Years 1975–1983" in *Ohio Politics,* eds. Alexander Lamis and Brian Usher, 2nd ed. (Kent: Kent State University Press, 2007), 146–147.
8. "Ohio Department of Rehabilitation and Correction: Executive Clemency," Department of Rehabilitation and Correction, accessed October 10, 2014, http://www.drc.state.oh.us/web/execclemency.htm
9. Alan Johnson, "Kasich Again Stingy with Clemencies," *Columbus Dispatch,* December 27, 2013, accessed October 18, 2014, http://www.dispatch.com/content/stories/local/2013/12/27/kasich-again-stingy-with-clemencies.html
10. Tim Miller, "The Celeste Era 1983-1991" in *Ohio Politics,* eds. Alexander Lamis and Brian Usher, 2nd ed. (Kent: Kent State University, 2007), 173–174.
11. Robert Higgs, "Hard-Charging Ways Bring Mike DeWine Leadership Praise, Criticism as Grandstander," *Plain Dealer,* May 19, 2013.
12. Joe Hallett "DeWine Backs Wider Religious Exemption for Birth Control Coverage," *Columbus Dispatch,* March 30, 2013, accessed October 11, 2014, http://www.dispatch.com/content/stories/local/2013/03/30/dewine-backs-wider-religious-exemption.html.
13. Jackie Borchardt, "Federal Court Orders Ohio Restore Early Voting Hours on 3 Days Before Election Day," *Plain Dealer,* June 12, 2014.

14. "Fiscal Distress," accessed June 13, 2014, https;//ohioauditor.gov/fiscaldistress .html.
15. Jennifer Smith Rodgers, "Auditor Targets 100 More Schools," *Columbus Dispatch,* January 13, 2013, accessed October 11, 2014, http://www.dispatch.com/content/stories/local/2013/01/13/auditor-targets-100-more-schools.html.
16. "Incentive Programs," JobsOhio, accessed October 13, 2014, http://jobs-ohio.com/funding/
17. Josh Goodman, "Economic Development Agencies Face New Scrutiny," *Stateline,* December 28, 2012.
18. Robert Higgs, "JobsOhio's Annual Report Touts Successes, but Also Draws Critics' Fire," *Plain Dealer,* March 5, 2014, accessed October 19, 2014, http://www.cleveland .com/open/index.ssf/2014/03/jobsohios_annual_report_touts.html
19. Joe Vardon, "Kasich Signs Bill to Close JobsOhio's Books," *Columbus Dispatch,* June 5, 2013, accessed October13, 2014, http://www.dispatch.com/content/stories/local/2013/06/05/bill-signed-to-close-jobsohios-books.html.
20. Joe Vardon, "Kasich Turning from Tax Credits" *Columbus Dispatch,* December 9, 2012, accessed October 13, 2014, http://www.dispatch.com/content/stories/local/2012/12/09/kasich-turning-from-tax-credits.html.
21. Dan Gearino, "93 State Development Deals Fall Short," *Columbus Dispatch,* December 14, 2012, accessed October 18, 2014, http://www.dispatch.com/content/stories/business/2012/12/14/93-state-development-deals-fall-short.html
22. Timothy Keen, OBM Director "Testimony of Director Timothy S. Keen, Office of Budget and Management, House Finance and Appropriations Committee," February 5, 2013, accessed October 13, 2014, http://ooga.org/wp-content/uploads/Keen Testimony_HouseFinanceCommittee-1.pdf.
23. Ibid.
24. National Federation of Independent Business et al. v. Sebelius, Secretary of Health and Human Services et al., 132 S.Ct 2566 (2012).
25. Keen, "Testimony of Directory Timothy S. Keen, Office of Budget and Management, House Finance and Appropriations Committee."
26. Daniel Vock, "Under Scrutiny, States Trim List of Bad Bridget," *Governing*, June 4, 2014, accessed October 19, 2014, http://www.governing.com/news/headlines/gov-under-scrutiny-states-trim-list-of-bad-bridges.html
27. "Mission and Commitments," The Public Utilities Commission of Ohio, accessed October 19, 2014, http://www.puco.ohio.gov/puco/index.cfm/about-the-commission/mission-and-commitments/#sthash.EL3ZATLA.dpbs
28. "Governor Signs Green Energy Freeze Legislation," *Gongwer Ohio* 83 (June 13, 2014): Report #114, Article #1.
29. Russ Kellet, *LSC Redbook Analysis of the Executive Budget Proposal Public Utilities Commission of Ohio,* February 2013, 3.
30. "Advisory Opinions 101," Ethics Commission, State of Ohio, accessed October 19, 2014, http://ethics.ohio.gov/advice/101.shtml
31. Legislative Services Commission, *Current Boards and Commissions,* accessed June 2012.

32. Ibid.
33. Gargan, "The Ohio Executive Branch," 414.
34. Ibid., 415.
35. Brandon Blackwell, "Ohio Senate Poised to Give Chiropractors Authority to Clear Young Athletes Who Suffer Head Injuries," *Cleveland Plain Dealer.* June 4, 2013.
36. Tiffany L. Parks, "Law Would Allow State to Act on Sunset Committee's Suggestions," *Akron Legal News,* July 1, 2011, accessed October 13, 2014, http://www.akronlegalnews.com/editorial/770

CHAPTER 5

Courts in Ohio

Introduction

The Ohio court system's roots extend back to the Northwest Ordinance of 1787. The territory covered by the ordinance was to be administered by a governor working with three judges. Although the judges were empowered to hear cases, they also served as quasi-legislators. Acting in that capacity, the second law that they approved formed what was called a *court of common pleas*, a term that is still used in Ohio. The law called for the appointing of between three and five judges in each county to this newly formed court. From those humble beginnings has evolved a complex court system that includes more than 700 elected judges who collectively process nearly three million cases each year.[1]

The threshold of the Ohio court system is a series of trial courts. These include municipal courts, county courts, common pleas courts, and even mayor's courts (see Figure 5.1). With a few exceptions, almost all cases in Ohio originate in one of these trial courts. Those who lose at the trial court level may appeal their case to an intermediate appeals court, known in Ohio as the *court of appeals*.[2] Finally, the court of last resort in Ohio is called the *supreme court*. The one unique feature of the Ohio court system—shared only by Louisiana—is that Ohio allows mayors in certain towns and cities to hold what are called *mayor's courts*. These courts are presided over by a mayor who is not required to have a law degree. He or she is required to receive specific training and usually hears cases involving the violation of local ordinances and traffic laws.

Magistrates

The late chief justice of the Ohio supreme court, Thomas Moyer, said that magistrates "are the face of the [Ohio] judiciary."[3] It is certainly true that many Ohioans who interact with the Ohio court system are likely to come before a magistrate

FIGURE 5.1 Ohio Court Structure

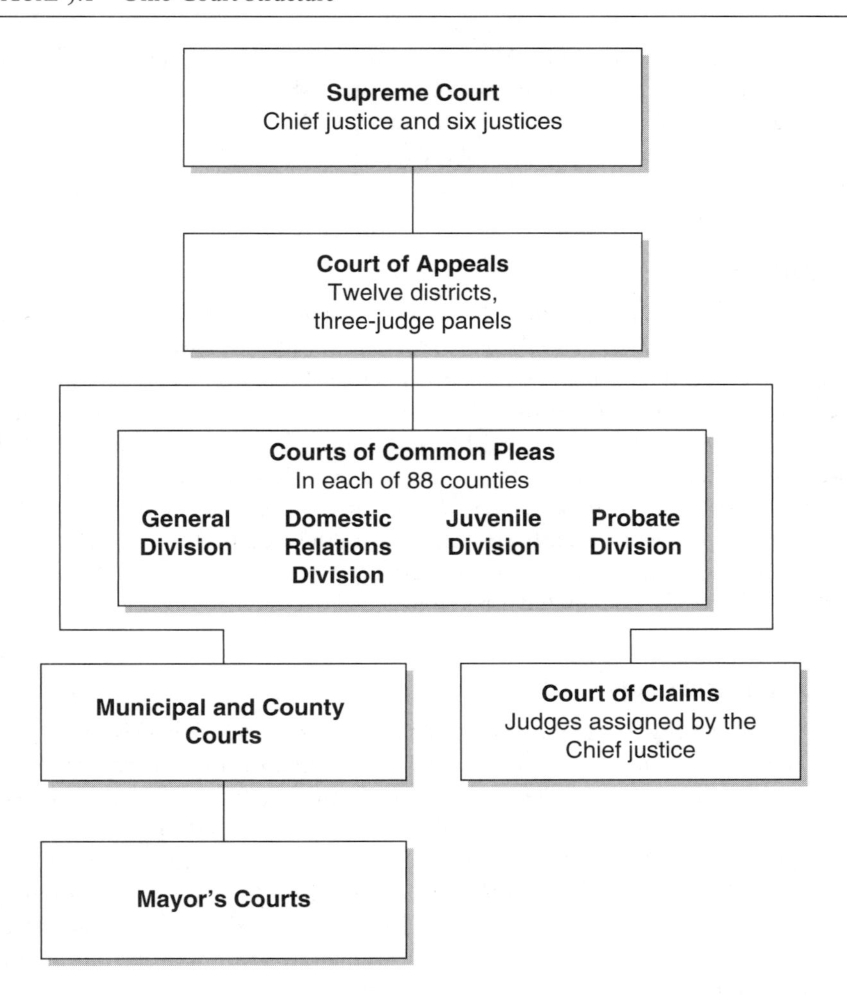

rather than a judge. Magistrates in Ohio, who before 1990 were called *referees*, perform activities normally associated with judges, such as conducting pretrial hearings, setting bail, and even conducting nonjury trials. Although magistrates can issue orders—for example, granting a continuance in a case—they cannot issue final judgments, and a judge must adopt decisions that they make before they become effective.

Although judges are not required to seek the assistance of magistrates, judges at every court level in Ohio have the power to appoint magistrates. In order to be qualified to serve, an individual is required to have practiced law for at least four years. There is no set term or salary for magistrates.

Currently, more than 800 magistrates work in the Ohio court system. Slightly over 60 percent of these are full-time magistrates. Magistrates may serve in more than one court and in several counties at the same time. In 2012, magistrates disposed of 363,115 cases. Nearly half of those cases were heard in one of the juvenile divisions of the court of common pleas.

Mayor's Courts

Municipal corporations in Ohio with populations greater than 200 may establish what are called a *mayor's court*. A mayor's court is only empowered to hear cases involving local ordinances and state traffic offenses. Local mayors who preside over these courts are not required to be lawyers but must receive some legal training. Currently, 318 municipal corporations in Ohio have a mayor's court. In 2012, these courts had an overall caseload that was over 300,000 cases.[4] Over three-quarters of these cases involved traffic violations. Since most potential cases are terminated by the accused simply paying a fine to the local traffic bureau, only 731 actual trials occurred in mayor's courts in 2012. Mayors themselves conducted 115 of these trials, with the remainder being presided over by magistrates.[5]

Municipal and County Courts

There are 35 county courts and 130 municipal courts in Ohio. These courts are the workhorses of the Ohio court system. In 2012, municipal courts were responsible for over 1.9 million cases, while county courts heard an additional 164,490 cases.[6] Both municipal and county courts are the creation of the Ohio legislature, relying on its power under Article IV of the state constitution to create inferior courts (that is, courts that are below the Ohio supreme court, court of appeals, and common pleas courts). In some counties, the state has only allowed for municipal courts, while in other counties, county courts have been authorized for geographical areas not covered by municipal courts. The jurisdiction (kinds of cases that a court may hear) of municipal and county courts is identical. These courts are empowered to hear criminal misdemeanor cases, traffic cases, and civil actions where the amount of money involved is less than $15,000. County court judges in Ohio serve part time, while municipal court judges may be either full time or part time.

Court of Common Pleas

Unlike the municipal and county courts, the court of common pleas of Ohio is established directly by the Ohio constitution and is the trial court that hears most serious cases in Ohio. Each of the 88 counties has a court of common pleas. In most counties, the court is divided into criminal and civil, domestic relations, juvenile, and probate divisions. The criminal and civil divisions handle criminal felony cases and civil cases involving more than $15,000. The domestic relations division of the court of common pleas hears marriage-related cases such as divorces, legal separations, and annulments. Judges assigned to the juvenile division of the courts of common pleas have exclusive jurisdiction over cases involving those under the age of 18, including cases where adults are accused of contributing to the delinquency of minors. Finally, the probate division is responsible for making determinations about wills and estates as well as determining such issues as legal guardianships and adoptions. The probate division also issues marriage licenses.

Court of Appeals

Those who are unhappy with the decision made at the municipal, county, or common pleas court level may appeal the decision to the court of appeals in their districts. There are the twelve courts of appeals, each representing a district that encompasses between one and 17 counties. The legislature establishes the districts and also determines, based on both population and caseload, the number of judges who will serve in each of the districts (see Map 5.1). The districts are not equal in population. The 4th District, for example, encompasses 633,838 people, while the 5th District is twice as large, with a population of 1,484,932. Currently, there are at least four and as many as twelve judges on each appeals court.

Court of appeals in Ohio exercises both appellate jurisdiction (the ability to hear a case on appeal from a lower court) and original jurisdiction (the ability to hear a case before any other court has rendered a decision). The court of appeals may exercise its original jurisdiction in cases where a party is seeking a writ of *quo warranto* (questioning a public official's right to their office or powers), *mandamus* (commanding a public official to perform a duty), *habeas corpus* (determining whether a prisoner is being legally held), *prohibition* (ordering a halt to proceedings beyond an lower court's legal authority), or *procedendo* (order to a lower court to proceed to a judgment) and, according to Article IV, Section 3 of the Ohio constitution, "[i]n any cause on review as may be necessary to its complete determination." These types of cases are rare, however, and compose a very small percentage of the cases heard by court of appeals in Ohio. On average, nearly half of the cases heard by court of appeals are appeals of lower court decisions in criminal cases.

Regardless of how many judges are on an individual court of appeals, randomly selected panels made up of only three of the judges hear cases. In a normal appeal, the three-judge panel looks at the lower court record and written briefs submitted by the parties to the controversy and also hears oral arguments from lawyers representing the litigants. A majority of at least two judges is necessary to

MAP 5.1 Ohio Court of Appeals Districts

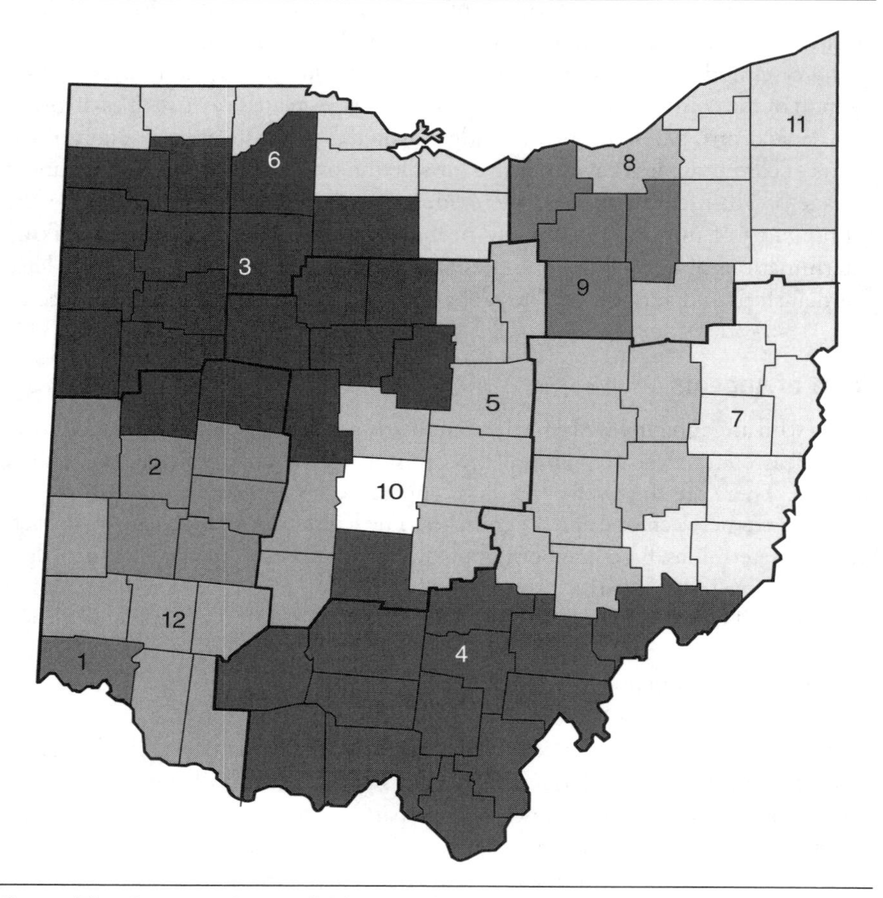

Source: The Supreme Court of Ohio & The Ohio Judicial System, "Ohio Courts of Appeals," accessed October 16, 2014, http://www.supremecourt.ohio.gov/judsystem/districtcourts/

decide a case. After a case is decided, the court produces a written opinion explaining the reasoning behind the conclusion. A judge on the panel who disagrees may write a dissenting opinion, explaining why he or she thinks that the case was wrongly decided. A court of appeals may issue several different types of decisions. The court may, for example, decide to overturn or uphold a decision made by a lower court. Alternatively, a court of appeals may determine that the decision of a lower court needs to be modified or that additional proceedings need to take place.

The Ohio Supreme Court

The supreme court of Ohio is the court of last resort in the Buckeye state. Formally established by Article IV, Section 2 of the Ohio constitution, the court has, since 1913, consisted of six justices and one chief justice (Photo 5.1). When deciding cases, the chief justice's vote carries no more weight than the vote of the remaining six justices. The chief justice does, however, have some additional administrative responsibilities, including appointing judges to the court of claims or to other courts when necessary.

The Supreme Court of Ohio

The Ohio Supreme Court Judges

Like the court of appeals, the Ohio supreme court is primarily a court of appellate jurisdiction. The supreme court's limited original jurisdiction mirrors that of the court of appeals discussed above. The only difference is that the supreme court is also empowered to hear, within its original jurisdiction, cases involving the practice of law, including disciplinary cases against lawyers.

The supreme court primarily hears cases that are brought to it from the court of appeal. Under the Ohio constitution, although the supreme court has discretion over which criminal and civil cases it chooses to hear, the court is required to grant review to the following cases: (1) cases that originate in the court of appeals, (2) cases in which the death penalty was affirmed, or (3) cases that involve a federal or state constitutional question. The court must also hear appeals from certain administrative agencies. In addition to deciding cases, the supreme court is responsible for adopting rules governing the Ohio courts.

In 2012, 2,187 cases were appealed to the supreme court. Of these cases, 1,629 were what are called *jurisdictional appeals*, meaning that the supreme court could decide whether or not to hear these cases. The court granted full review to 82 (or about 5 percent) of these appeals.[7]

The supreme court normally hears cases in the state capital of Columbus. Since 1987, however, as part of the Off-Site Court Program, the Ohio supreme court holds hearings twice a year in different counties around the state. The court hears arguments on Tuesday and Wednesday mornings, with formal written opinions also being announced on Wednesdays. A lottery system is used to determine which justice (including the chief justice) will be assigned to write the opinion that represents a majority (at least four members) of the court. Numbered balls, corresponding to each of the justices voting with the majority—and the chief justice, if he or she is part of the majority—are placed in a bottle with a top narrow enough to allow only one ball at a time to escape. The justice who voted with the majority who has served on the court for the longest period of time (the "senior justice") tilts the bottle to release a ball. The justice or chief justice whose number corresponds with the number on the ball is assigned to write the opinion. So that all of the justices are assigned a similar number of opinions, that particular numbered ball is not reused until everyone on the court has been assigned an opinion.[8]

Court of Claims

The Ohio general assembly created the court of claims in 1975. The court of claims hears cases involving civil claims against the state of Ohio. Unlike other courts in Ohio, the court of claims does not have permanent judges. The court does have a clerk and deputy clerk, and these officials decide cases in which claims are in the amount of $10,000 or less. If the decision of clerk or deputy clerk is appealed or if the amount in question is more than $10,000, either a judge or a panel of judges (in very complex cases) appointed by the chief justice of the Ohio supreme court hears the case.

The court of claims also hears appeals from the decisions of the Ohio attorney general's office in cases where claims have been made under the Victims of Crimes Act. The chief justice also appoints a panel of three commissioners who hear the initial appeals in these cases. The commissioners serve six-year terms. A final appeal from a decision by the commissioners may be taken to court of claims judge.

Judicial Selection in Ohio

Under the state's first constitution, judges in Ohio were to be elected by the general assembly. When, in 1851, a new constitution was adopted, it made several changes to Ohio judiciary, including providing for the popular election of judges. Ohio is now one of 21 states that allow voters to select their judges at the polls.[9]

Although Ohio has elected its judges for more than 160 years, the process has undergone some changes. Originally, the political parties nominated judges through various methods, including party conventions. The party affiliation of the judge was then listed on the general election ballot. In 1911, the general assembly passed the Nonpartisan Judiciary Act, which ordered the party affiliation of judges to be removed from the ballot.[10] The next year, the Ohio constitution was amended to mandate that the political parties use primaries to select their standard bearers. In practice, this means that judges in Ohio are selected in partisan political primaries and therefore generally must run as Democrats or Republicans. General election voters, however, are not provided with any information on the ballot about the political affiliation of the judicial candidates nominated by the parties. Now, because judges are expected to decide cases in a nonpartisan manner, the use of nonpartisan ballots is not unusual in the United States. Among the states that elect judges, all but seven ban the inclusion of party affiliation on the ballot. Ohio is the only state, however, that combines a nonpartisan general election ballot with partisan primary election system.

The judges and justices, including the chief justice of the Ohio supreme court, are elected to six-year terms. Municipal court judges are elected during odd-numbered years, while all other judges appear on the ballot in even-numbered years. All judges, including the chief justice and justices of the supreme court, can be removed from office by a vote of two-thirds of both houses of the general assembly. If a vacancy occurs on any court, the governor is empowered to make a temporary appointment.

BOX 5.1: Ohio Chief Justice Proposes Changes to Judicial Selection

In May of 2013, the chief justice of the Ohio supreme court, Maureen O'Connor issued a 26-page document entitled "A Proposal for Strengthening Judicial Elections."[1] Relying on a recent study that demonstrated that elected judges were no less qualified than appointed judges, the chief justice did not advocate for the elimination of judicial elections in Ohio. Instead, she suggested ways that judicial elections might be reformed to increase public confidence in the Ohio courts as well as encourage more participation in judicial elections. Although not advocating for any particular change, the chief justice recommended that the following proposals be discussed:

1. *Rotate Ballot Order*: Nonpartisan elections are placed at the end of what are sometimes quite long Ohio ballots. Voters, perhaps out of fatigue, tend not to complete their ballots and therefore do not participate in judicial elections. The proposal suggests that rotating the order of positions on the ballot might solve this problem, allowing judicial elections to, at times, hold a more prominent place on the ballot.

2. *Hold All Judicial Elections during Odd-Numbered Years*: Currently, only municipal judges are elected during odd-numbered years. The problem with holding judicial elections during even-numbered years is that judicial candidates must compete with congressional, state legislative, and either gubernatorial or

(Continued)

(Continued)

presidential candidates for attention. Holding elections during odd-numbered years would essentially clear the decks for candidates running for a judicial position.

3. *Provide More Information about Judicial Candidates*: A 2003 League of Women Voters survey found that only 4 percent of Ohioans could name even one member of the Ohio supreme court. Also, the data show that most voters feel they do not have enough information about judicial candidates to make an informed choice. This lack of information may be one of the reasons that voters do not vote in judicial elections. The proposal suggests the benefits of providing information through voter guides as well as by encouraging televised debates for judicial candidates.

4. *Hold Nonpartisan Judicial Primary Elections*: Among those states that elect judges, Ohio is unique in having partisan primaries and nonpartisan general elections. This creates an awkward system within which partisanship is real (judges must run in party primaries) but hidden from general election voters. The proposal suggests a more straightforward nonpartisan election system, with primaries (where parties choose candidates) being eliminated.

5. *Establish a Nonpartisan Nomination Commission to Fill Judicial Vacancies*: A majority of the judges and justices in Ohio initially gain their seats on the bench by being appointed by the governor to fill a vacancy. Although governors do solicit nominations from local political parties, the proposal would create nonpartisan nominating commissions that might be able to draw from a larger and more diverse group of qualified candidates.

6. *Require Those Appointed by the Governor to be Confirmed by the Ohio Senate*: Currently, the governor is able to unilaterally fill vacancies on the state bench. Given the importance of the appointments, it might be wise to follow the model used for federal appointments under the U.S. Constitution and mandate that judicial nominees be subject to the advice and consent of the Ohio senate.

7. *Increase Judicial Qualifications*: In Ohio, lawyers must have practiced law for at least six years prior to being considered qualified for any judgeship in the state. Lengthening this requirement, particularly for those who seek to serve on courts in the municipal or county court levels, might be appropriate insofar as more experienced lawyers might instill more confidence in the system.

8. *Increase the Length of Judicial Terms*: The current term of six years for all judges in Ohio may be too short to allow judges to feel insulated from public opinion and therefore able to render decisions that are truly independent. Lengthening terms—including a 12-year term for supreme court justices under the proposal—would allow judges and justices at least temporary freedom from electoral constraints.

Note

1. Maureen O'Connor, *A Proposal for Strengthening Judicial Elections,* accessed October 16, 2014, http://ohiojudicialreform.org/wp-content/resources/Plan13.pdf

Problems and Proposals

Throughout the years, various groups have expressed dissatisfaction with the manner in which Ohio chooses those who sit on the bench. First of all, elections are expensive. Since 2000, candidates for the supreme court in Ohio have spent over 18 million dollars on their campaigns. In 2012 alone, nearly 4 million dollars was spent on the three supreme court contests on the ballot.[11] The sheer amount of money spent of judicial elections raises questions about judicial independence. "Just what," one may ask, "are donors trying to buy?" One of the problems is that on high-profile issues such as the constitutionality of Ohio's system for funding primary and secondary education or legislative proposals to limit the amount of damages awarded by a jury to those who have been injured, the major political parties have clear positions on what they think the Ohio constitution demands. Since Ohio has partisan primary elections for judicial posts, those who have an interest in the outcomes of these cases are provided with a major clue as to how a judge or justice is likely to rule in these areas. Donations can be seen as an attempt to push the court toward a particular reading of the state's constitution. At the same time, it costs quite of bit of money to run for a court, in particular, the Ohio supreme court. Therefore, the only way to limit the apparent influence of money is to do away with judicial elections.

There have been several attempts to amend the Ohio constitution to change how judicial selection takes place in Ohio. These revisions, which often call for gubernatorial appointments from a list of candidates prescreened by an independent panel, are usually referred to as *Missouri plans*. This is because Missouri, in 1940, was the first state whose voters approved such a judicial selection system. Given Ohio's influence on national politics, it is interesting to note that a merit selection proposal was offered in Ohio in 1938, two years before Missouri passed its plan. The proposed 1938 amendment was virtually identical to the plan adopted two years later in Missouri. The amendment called for all appellate court judges (judges on the court of appeals and the justices and the chief justice of the Ohio supreme court) to be nominated by the governor from among a slate of individuals recommended by an eight-member judicial council. The nomination would be subject to a confirmation vote in the senate. After a term in office, the judge would have to go before the voters. There would, however, be no opponent and the voters would only be casting their ballots on the question of whether to retain the judge in office.

Ohio voters overwhelmingly rejected the 1938 amendment. In the years since, many plans have been put forward in Ohio similar to the merit plan of 1938. In 1968, voters in Ohio approved what was summarized as the *Modern Courts Amendment*. The amendment made several additions to the Ohio constitution, for example, strengthening the leadership role of the Ohio supreme court over other courts in the state.[12] Originally, the proposed set of changes included a merit selection provision. The Ohio house of representatives removed this provision before the ballot measure was placed before the voters.[13] The most serious attempt took place in 1987, when a proposal was placed on the Ohio ballot that would have established merit panels for each of the appellate districts and the state supreme court. These panels would, as in the 1938 proposal, recommended candidates for nomination by the governor. The near 2–1 margin of defeat for the 1987 ballot measure was nearly identical to the 1938 vote.[14] More recently, a poll showed that over 80 percent of Ohioans want to keep voting for judges—or at least, for supreme court justices.[15]

There are many other problems that have been identified with judicial elections in Ohio besides the possible corrupting role of money in judicial campaigns. First, there is a question about how much information voters have about judicial candidates. This lack of information may lead to what is sometimes called the "name game" when it comes to elections for the Ohio supreme court. For example, over the past 50 years, seven different members of the Ohio supreme court have shared the surname "Brown."[16] In addition, studies have found that there is a significant drop off as voters work their way down the ballot to arrive at the judicial candidates (Figure 5.2). This means that many voters do not participate in judicial elections.

Finally, despite all the discussions about judicial elections, more than half of the judges serving in Ohio first gain their position by gubernatorial appointment. Given the natural advantage that incumbents have on the ballot, this represents a rather important and unchecked power granted to the Ohio governor.

Conclusion

Ohio's court system has much in common with those used in a majority of the states. Its basic structure mirrors that used by the federal government and in most of the states. Even in electing its judges, Ohio is really not unusual. Many states follow this

FIGURE 5.2 Supreme Court Race Voter Drop Off, 2002–2012

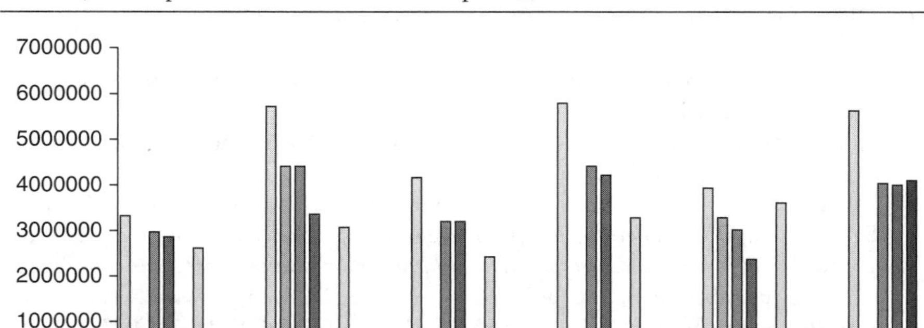

Source: Maureen O'Connor, *A Proposal for Strengthening Judicial Elections*, accessed October 17, 2014, http://ohiojudicialreform.org/wp-content/resources/Plan13.pdf

system. Despite all of this, the Ohio court system does exhibit some unique features. For example, Ohio maintains mayor's courts in some cities and combines partisan primaries with nonpartisan general elections. The chief justice of the Ohio supreme court, Maureen O'Connor, has questioned this latter system, which does not exist in any other state. As discussed in Chapter 2, it was dissatisfaction with the court system that led Ohioans to write a new constitution in 1851. While a new constitutional convention in Ohio is unlikely, at least for another two decades (when the question will have to be put once again to Ohio voters), the Ohio Constitutional Modernization Commission is currently meeting. One of its committees has indicated it will "consider issues concerning judicial election or appointment."[17]

Notes

1. Ohio Supreme Court, *Ohio Courts Statistical Summary 2012*, p. 7, accessed October 15, 2014, http://www.supremecourt.ohio.gov/Publications/annrep/12OCS/summary/trend.pdf
2. Appeals from a mayor's court would go to the municipal or county court rather than to the courts of appeals.
3. Chief Justice Thomas Moyer, "Address at New Magistrate Orientation," March 24, 2010.
4. Ohio Supreme Court, *2012 Mayor's Courts Summary*, accessed October 16, 2014, http://www.supremecourt.ohio.gov/Publications/mayorscourt/mayorscourtssummary12.pdf

5. Ibid.
6. Ohio Supreme Court, *Ohio Courts Statistical Summary 2012*, 7.
7. Ibid., 12.
8. "The Supreme Court of Ohio," accessed October 16, 2014, http://www.legislature.state.oh.us/judicial.cfm
9. "Judicial Selection in the States," American Judicature Society, accessed October 16, 2014, http://www.judicialselection.us.
10. Michael Solimine, Carolyn Chavez, Thomas Pulley, and Lee Sprouse, "Judicial Selection in Ohio: History, Recent Developments, and an Analysis of Reform Proposals," *Report of the Center for Law and Justice at the University of Cincinnati College of Law*, September 2003, p. 6, accessed October 16, 2014, http://www.lwvohio.org/assets/attachments/file/JUDICIAL%20SELECTION%20IN%20OHIO_%20HISTORY,%20RECENT.pdf
11. Alicia Bannon, Eric Velasco, Linda Casey, and, Lianda Reagan, "State Profiles, 2011–2012, Ohio, Contested Election," *The New Politics of Judicial Elections Online, Appendix*, accessed October 16, 2014, http://newpoliticsreport.org/report/2012-report/appendix/
12. Maureen O'Connor, "The Ohio Modern Courts Amendment: 45 Years of Progress," *Albany Law Review* 76, issue 4 (2013): 1968.
13. William T. Milligan and James E. Pohlman, "The 1968 Modern Courts Amendment to the Ohio Constitution," *Ohio State Law Journal* 29 (1968): 817.
14. Solimine et al., "Judicial Selection in Ohio: History, Recent Developments, and an Analysis of Reform Proposals," 10.
15. "Quinnipiac Poll," Quinnipiac University, December 12, 2012, accessed October 17, 2014, http://www.quinnipiac.edu/institutes-and-centers/polling-institute/ohio/release-detail?ReleaseID=1823
16. "'Name Game' Rules Again in Ohio Supreme Court Races: Editorial," *Plain Dealer*, November 7, 2012, accessed October 17, 2014, http://www.cleveland.com/opinion/index.ssf/2012/11/name_game_rules_again_in_ohio.html
17. Ohio Constitutional Modernization Commission,*Report of Judicial Branch and Administration of Justice Committee,* July 11, 2013, accessed October 17, 2014, http://www.ocmc.ohio.gov/ocmc//uploads/Judicial%20Branch%20and%20Administration%20of%20Justice%20Committee/2013-07-11%20Judicial%20Branch%20Committee%20Report.doc

CHAPTER 6

Local Government in Ohio

Local government in Ohio has its origins in the Land Ordinance of 1785. Passed by the continental Congress to prepare for the sale of this land, this ordinance proposed surveying the western lands into six-mile square townships. In the Ohio territory, a five-mile square was often substituted for the six-mile square township. In 1804, after Ohio became a state, the general assembly decided to create civil townships throughout Ohio. When the population of the townships reached 80, the residents could form a township government. The powers and duties of townships decreased over the decades as more and more counties were created by the Ohio legislature. Local political subdivisions in Ohio now include counties, townships, villages, and cities.

County Government

The state of Ohio gradually increased the number of county governments until it reached the current number of 88. The county is an agent of state government and the state statutes specifically spell out the structure and the duties of the counties. There are three elected commissioners in each county in Ohio. Two commissioners are elected in the year of the presidential election and the third during the midterm election year. They are elected for four-year terms and have both legislative and executive authority. The authority of the commissioners, however, is limited by statute and by the fact that there are numerous separately elected county officials, including prosecutor, sheriff, auditor, coroner, treasurer, clerk of courts, county engineer, and the county recorder. This county form of government for counties has long been seen as inefficient and outdated by government reformers in Ohio. County governments in Ohio rely on the piggyback sales tax for a significant portion their revenue. *Piggyback* means that the county sales tax is on top of the state sales tax and is collected with it. The lion's share of Ohio's county government budgets goes to public safety, which includes the sheriff's department, the courts, and the county jail (see Figure 6.1)

FIGURE 6.1 2014 General Fund Expenditures for Franklin County, Ohio

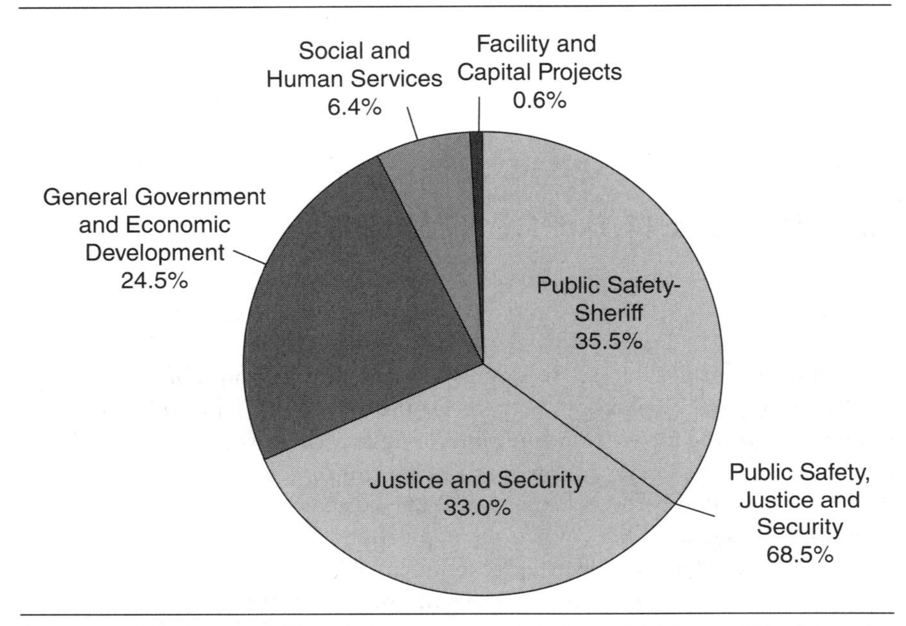

Source: Franklin County Office of Management and Budget, *2014 Approved Budget Packet*, http://budget.franklincountyohio.gov/budget/2014/pdf/budget-overview.pdf

Ohio Townships

There are 1,308 townships in Ohio and they provide limited local government services for citizens who do not reside in an incorporated municipality. The Ohio constitution provides for a township government and for the general assembly to provide for its form and powers of general law. Townships can only exercise those powers delegated to them by the general assembly. A three-member board of trustees governs townships. Two are elected in one odd year and the third is elected in the next odd year. Trustees enjoy a four-year term in office and may be reelected. The trustees have both legislative and executive authority, although it is quite limited and prescribed by state law. The fiscal officer, formerly called the *clerk*, is also elected in the year the single trustee is elected. All of these elected township officials are elected in nonpartisan elections, and there is no primary to limit the number of candidates. Those with the highest vote totals are elected.

The only way for townships to earn their own revenue is by imposing property tax levies that are voted on by the residents. Township governments exercise basic functions such as maintenance of roads and ditches, operating a cemetery, fire protection, and zoning (if the residents adopt it). The governments can provide for police protection if they provide the needed financial support with a levy; otherwise, the responsibility for policing the township, as with many other functions, will default to the county.

In 1991, the state legislature provided the more populated townships the opportunity to opt for limited self-government. Even if this was adopted by the voters of the township, however, the grant of authority was very limited, including only such things as resolutions against barking dogs and fines for not cleaning up trash. There are some townships in Ohio with sizable populations, and there is statutory language for these townships to incorporate themselves as cities with a charter. State law makes this choice unattractive, however, because the newly formed city would have to take over a number of responsibilities previously carried by the county government without charge to the township. Very few Ohio townships have incorporated in recent decades because of the additional costs to their residents.

Ohio Municipal Government

According to the U.S. Census of Governments, there are 938 municipalities in Ohio. This includes cities and villages both chartered and statutory. In the early years of the Ohio municipal government, the general assembly granted special acts for the incorporation of each municipality. The state legislature individually chartered each municipality by a special act. The legislature provided for the form, organization, and structure of the municipality.[1] The municipalities were not all treated alike. The constitution of 1851 changed that and provided that "[t]he General Assembly shall provide for the organization of cities and incorporated villages by general laws. . . . The General Assembly shall pass no special act conferring corporate powers."[2] Municipalities were to be subject to general laws applicable to all municipalities. The current classification of municipalities in use is a result of a 1912 amendment to the Ohio constitution that states, in part,

> Municipal corporations are hereby classified into cities and villages. All such corporations having a population of five thousand or over shall be cities; all others shall be villages. The method of transition from one class to the other shall be regulated by law.[3]

The authority of municipal government in Ohio is defined by Article XVIII of the state constitution, which was enacted as a constitutional amendment initiated by the Ohio Constitutional Convention of 1912. Article XVIII states, "Municipalities shall have authority to exercise all powers of local self-government and to adopt and enforce within their limits such local police, sanitary and other similar regulations, as are not in conflict with general laws."

The Process of Incorporation

Village

The land area of a proposed new village must be at least two square miles and have a population of at least 800 persons per square mile. It must also have an assessed property valuation of $3,500 per capita. A petition must be signed by a majority of the registered voters living in the area to be incorporated and then presented to the county commissioners. The county commissioners hold a hearing during which people can speak for or against the incorporation. If the commissioners decide in favor of the petitioner, the incorporation becomes effective when notification is given to the secretary of state. Officers are elected in the next election. This process is more complex if there is an existing municipality within three miles of the proposed new village.[4] In Ohio, a village becomes a city if its population climbs over 5,000.

City

Incorporation of a new city requires at least four square miles and each square mile must have a population of at least 1,000 people. The total population must be at least 25,000 and the assessed valuation of property must be at least $2,500 per capita. A petition must be signed by at least 20 percent of the electors of the territory. This application must then be presented to the county commissioners. If the county commissioners find everything in order, the issue is placed on the ballot. Voters in the affected area then determine if they wish to incorporate the new city. Legislation established in 1967 made it more difficult for townships to incorporate, with the expectation that townships would be annexed by nearby cities. That has not occurred and townships have pushed back in the legislature for more governing authority.

Organizing the Municipality

Ohio law provides alternative measures that incorporated villages and cities may use to organize their local government. The first is the statutory form, where the municipality, by not adopting its own charter, defaults to the municipal organization defined in state statute. A municipality can also, however, decide to follow the state statutory procedures to create a charter and determine its own form of government.

Statutory Form

The statutory form used most frequently provides for a strong mayor/council organization in Ohio cities and a weak mayor/council plan for villages.[5] Partisan elections are required for cities and nonpartisan elections for villages. A city council, under the statutory plan, consists of not less than seven members, four of whom shall be elected by wards and three at large. A sliding scale based on population provides for the addition or loss of council members for a city. City council members in a statutory municipality have only legislative authority. The executive power is vested in a mayor, auditor, treasurer, president of council, and director of law, all of whom are elected. Very few cities actually use the statutory form, with fairly large cities of Canton and Warren being notable exceptions. Most large cities in Ohio have adopted their own charter.

Ohio villages often use the statutory form. A village that uses the statutory form has a village council of six members elected at large to four-year overlapping terms. The village council has both legislative and administrative powers. Villages may create the position of village administrator by ordinance. If created, the administrator serves as the administrative head of village utility and street functions.

Charter Form

The Ohio constitution provides that Ohio cities and villages can use home rule authority to adopt charters that vary the form of municipal government. Under Article XVIII of the Ohio constitution (Section 7 [Home Rule]), "Any municipality may frame and adopt or amend a charter for its government and may, subject to the provisions of section 3 of this article, exercise there under all powers of local self-government."[6] Section 3 of Article XVIII of the Ohio constitution states, "Municipalities shall have authority to exercise all powers of local self-government and to adopt and enforce within their limits such local police, sanitary and other similar regulations, as are not in conflict with general laws."

Where a charter has been adopted, the provisions of the charter control matters of structure and organization of the municipality. The procedure to adopt a city charter involves two steps. The first is to place the question of whether or not to consider adopting a charter before the voters. In the same election, a 15-member commission is elected to frame a charter. This initial question can be placed before the voters by a two-thirds vote of the city council. Alternatively, the council can be obligated to place the question on the ballot by a petition of 10 percent of the city electors. The second step is for the commission to write a charter that will then be placed before the voters. If approved, the charter becomes the governing document of the municipality. The vote to approve the charter must occur within one year after the election of the charter commission.[7]

The charter is a legal instrument that resembles a constitution for the municipal government. In theory, use of a charter does not expand the scope of municipal power, but it does provide the opportunity to be responsive to local needs rather than rely on the general assembly, as is the case with the statutory form. According to the Ohio Municipal League,

> The purpose of Article XVIII, Section 7 of the Ohio Constitution is to permit local citizens to provide their own form of government and their own procedures which meet their approval and meet their needs in a manner that may be different from those provided under state law.[8]

As of 1995, there were 173 cities and 51 villages with charters in Ohio.

There are a variety of forms of local self-government that a charter commission can create. The strong mayor form speaks to the power of the mayor, not the personal characteristics of a particular mayor. In this form, the mayor is elected and appoints department heads, commission members, and other administrators, often without city council approval. Also in this form, the mayor is granted a veto power. This form meets the goals of the early reformers, who promoted the short ballot with fewer elected officials. That was designed to enable the public to hold a few officials accountable.

Under the weak mayor form, executive authority is divided among other elected officials such as a law director, treasurer, and auditor. Also, the mayor's appointments to boards and commissions are subject to council confirmation. Frequently under this form, the mayor does not have veto power. Proponents of this model argue that it provides for checks and balances, since there is no concentration of power. This is quite similar to the statutory form provided for non-charter cities.

The city manager plan has the city council as the primary policy maker for the city. The council appoints the executive head of the municipality, who serves at the pleasure of the council. This manager usually appoints the major department heads such as law, finance, safety, and service. In some instances, the appointments are subject to council approval. The manager does not vote on legislation and is not given veto power. The president of the city council frequently performs the ceremonial duties for the city and is often given the title of mayor. The emphasis in this city model is professionalism and a de-emphasis of politics in city affairs. Cincinnati was one of the largest cities in the nation to adopt a city manager form. Recently, it enhanced the office of the mayor but retained the city manager, so it is deemed a stronger mayor form.[9]

Under the commission plan, the number of commissioners is three or five members, and they have both legislative and executive authority. The county commissioners and the township trustees are modified forms of the commission form, altered for use in Ohio.[10] The commission plan is rarely used in Ohio. The one exception may be the city of Dayton. On its website, Dayton claims it was the first large city in the United States to adopt the city manager form of government, and the Ohio Municipal League classifies the city as having what it identifies as a commission–manager form of government.[11] Dayton has a five-member commission elected at large. One of the commissioners is separately elected as the mayor of that city.

There are other provisions in a city charter that impact the performance of the municipality, such as the term and possible term limits of the elected officials. The compensation of the officials also might be stated in the charter or charter amendments. Recall for the mayor is provided in some charters. Charters will also determine the number of city council members and whether they will be elected using partisan or nonpartisan ballots as well as whether they will be elected from wards, at large, or a mixture of both. Incorporated chartered cities can regularly create charter commissions, which might offer charter amendments that are then placed before the voters for adoption. Municipalities have no power, by charter or otherwise, to create courts or appoint judges because that power is vested in the general assembly.[12] The Ohio constitution reserves the right of initiative and referendum to the people of each municipality.[13]

The Path to Local Government Reform

The city of Cincinnati has long been interested in political reform. In the early 20th century, the city was under the influence of Republican Party boss George Cox, who operated an effective political machine. Cox's clout was dependent on his ability to dispense patronage. It was Cox's view that "the man who makes possible the nomination should be first considered when favors are passed around."[14] Democratic victories in Cincinnati in 1911, along with charges of corruption, led to a split within the Republican Party. Civic activists took advantage of this situation to form the Charter Party in Cincinnati, whose goal it was to dismantle Cox's political machine. In 1926, this movement led to a new municipal charter for Cincinnati and the creation of a council-manager form of city government. In response to Boss Cox's control, Cincinnati moved from a ward council system to an at-large system of nine council members. At the time, it was assumed by the progressive reformers that this would make it more difficult for political machines to nominate and control council members. Concerns have been raised about the effect that at-large elections may have on minority representation on city council. The council-manager form has, in recent years, been changed into what some have termed a *stronger mayor* form of government, and the first "stronger mayor" elected in Cincinnati was Mark Mallory, an African American.

The Cincinnati-based reform groups collaborated with reform groups around the state and submitted by initiative petition an amendment to Article X of the Ohio state constitution. Among other things, this amendment permitted Ohio counties to adopt a charter for government.[15] The constitutional amendment was adopted in 1933, and since then, the movement for counties to incorporate and adopt a charter has moved at a snail's pace. A few counties have taken on a new form. In the late 1970s, Summit County changed to a council and executive form of county government and eliminated some of the countywide elected offices. This governmental reform occurred because of a scandal involving a judge and the conviction of a number of other Summit County public officials on charges of public corruption.

Recently, Cuyahoga County was subject to a lengthy Federal Bureau of Investigation (FBI) examination into public corruption, which led to the conviction of a number of county officials in federal court. To remove this scent of corruption, Cuyahoga County voters supported a county charter form of government, with an elected executive and an 11-member county council. Only the county prosecutor remained as a separately elected position. Beyond Summit and Cuyahoga counties, none of the remaining 86 counties in Ohio have opted to take advantage of a charter government.

BOX 6.1: Charter Reform in Cuyahoga County, Ohio

Political scandal, the same force that drove charter reform in Summit County decades earlier, recently prompted a similar reform movement in Cuyahoga County. The seeds of the Cuyahoga County charter reform were planted in July of 2008, when 200 FBI and Internal Revenue Service (IRS) agents raided Cuyahoga County offices, businesses, and homes connected to two of the most powerful political figures in the county, Commissioner and Democratic Party Chairman Jimmy Dimora and County Auditor Frank Russo. The FBI brought in support personnel from Pittsburgh and needed three U-Haul trucks to haul documents and evidence.[1] There were lists of charges, including free work by contractors who, in exchange, received county contract work as well as sexual favors. Eventually, in September of 2010, this resulted in an indictment directed at Dimora and his political cronies—including some area judges—that ran 177 pages in length.

The drumbeat of local government corruption news led to the emergence of a county reform movement called "New Cuyahoga Now." Cuyahoga County Prosecutor Bill Mason and Parma Heights Mayor Martin Zanotti, who was also chairman of the Northeast Ohio Mayors and City Managers Association, led the group. New Cuyahoga Now proposed a charter giving the county home rule authority, including the ability to establish a new form of government and pass ordinances.

This group decided to circumvent the election of a county charter commission and use the language in the Ohio Revised Code 307.94: "A county charter to be submitted to the voters by petition shall be considered to be attached to the petition if it is printed as a part of the petition."[2] They collected 81,000 signatures, 46,000 of which were ruled to be valid.[3] This met the statutorily required 10 percent of vote cast in the county in the last gubernatorial election.

The reformers faced several obstacles. Mayor Zanotti, though a lifetime Democrat, was potentially suspect in the eyes of other party members in Cuyahoga County because his brother, David, was the head of the conservative Ohio roundtable. Leaders of the African American community in Cuyahoga County were also hesitant about joining the reform because they were unsure of how African Americans would fare in this new government. Senator Nina Turner did support the reform efforts, but she was one of only a few African American elected officials in the county to take this position.[4]

There was also opposition from those who tried to cling to power, such as the remaining and untainted incumbent county commissioners, Tim Hagan and Peter Lawson Jones. Hagan and Jones, who were to be put out of office if the proposed reforms were put in place, attempted to create a diversion by offering a ballot proposition creating an elected charter commission to continue to study a new charter.[5] Their proposition was offered at the same election that voters were asked to adopt the reform charter submitted by the Mason-Zanotti group.

Despite all of these hurdles, the momentum for reform increased, fueled by the constant reports of political scandal throughout the county. The reform proposal, which was identified as Issue 6, was approved by 66 percent of the votes cast in the November 2009 election.[6] At the same time, the sitting commissioners' proposition to delay reform by further study went down to defeat.

The new form of county government included a single executive and an 11-member council elected from individual districts. All of the other county offices, except the county prosecutor, were eliminated, and their functions distributed to appointed offices defined in the new charter. The county executive would nominate the appointees, and the 11-member county council would have to confirm the nominations.[7] A general election for these positions was held on November 2, 2010, and those elected took the reins of the new government on January 1, 2011. The mayor of Lakewood, Edward FitzGerald (who would serve as the Democratic candidate for governor in 2014), was the Democratic Party nominee for the newly created office of county executive. He defeated the Republican nominee, Matt Dolan.

Notes

1. "Federal Raids Target Cuyahoga County Commissioner Jimmy Dimora, Cuyahoga County Auditor Frank Russo," *The Plan Dealer*, July 28, 2008, accessed

(Continued)

(Continued)

October 17, 2014, http://blog.cleveland.com/metro/2008/07/federal_raids_target_cuyahoga.html

2. This was the same path taken in Summit County's successful adoption of a charter. See Frank J. Kendrick, "A Charter for Summit County" in *Government and Politics in Ohio,* ed. Carl Lieberman (Lanham: University Press of America, 1974).
3. Mark Vosburgh, "Proposal for a New Form of Cuyahoga County Government Gets on November Ballot," *Cleveland.com,* July 20, 2009, accessed February 24, 2013.
4. Amanda Garrett, "How Cuyahoga County Reform Effort Turned into Political Turmoil," *Plain Dealer,* September 13, 2009, accessed October 17, 2014, http://blog.cleveland.com/metro/2009/09/how_cuyahoga_county_reform_eff.html
5. Ibid.
6. *Report of Votes Cast on Misc. Questions for the General Election Held on November 3, 2009,* comp. Jennifer Brunner, accessed October 18, 2014, http://www.sos.state.oh.us/sos/upload/elections/2009/gen/misc.pdf
7. "Cuyahoga County Charter," Country Charter Transition Advisory Group, accessed October 18, 2014, http://charter.cuyahogacounty.us/en-us/charter.aspx

Ohio's Major Cities

Ohio's major cities and their populations are displayed in Table 6.1 below. Ohio's cities, although they remain large population centers, have—for the most part—lost significant population over recent decades. Table 6.1 shows the decline for the cities according to the census. Only the city of Columbus has grown because it has long pursued annexation; its boundaries now extend beyond the boundaries of its home county, Franklin County. It pursued this expansion by refusing to provide water and sewer services unless the neighboring jurisdictions seeking these services agreed to annex to the city of Columbus.

The population of the city of Columbus, according to the 2010 census as displayed in Table 6.1, was 787,033—a 10.6 percent increase over 2000. One reason for the growth in population of Columbus compared to the other major Ohio cites is their aggressive use of annexation. Annexation is a legal process by which some property in an unincorporated area such as a township becomes part of a neighboring city or village. The property needs to be contiguous to qualify for annexation.[16] The most common scenario is that the property owner will seek to have their property annexed. The city of Columbus maintained tight control over its water and sewer services, according to former Columbus Mayor Buck Rinehart. He said that since the 1950s, under Mayor Jack Sensenbrenner, the city has

TABLE 6.1 Populations of Major Cities in Ohio

City	*Population 2000*	*Population 2010*
Akron	217,074	199,110
Cincinnati	331,285	296,943
Cleveland	478,403	396,815
Columbus	711,470	787,033
Dayton	166,179	141,527
Toledo	313,619	287,208

Data source: "American Fact Finder," United States Census Bureau, accessed October 23, 2014, Factfinder2.census.gov/faces/nav/jsf/pages/community_facts.xhtml

required annexation before it will provide water and sewer services.[17] One notable example of the expansion of the city boundary of Columbus is the privately developed Polaris Centers of Commerce, which expands into Delaware County, Ohio, and was annexed to Columbus to acquire water and sewer services. Columbus annexed it during the construction of the privately funded interchanges on Interstate 71.

Home Rule

The grant of home rule, stated as "authority to exercise all power of local self-government and to adopt and enforce within their limits such local police, sanitary and other similar regulations, as are not in conflict with general laws," has continuously been litigated in court in Ohio. There are, for example, often questions regarding the authority of an Ohio city that has adopted a charter, particularly when there is a conflict between a city ordinance or charter amendment and what is termed the general law of the state of Ohio. These conflicts are ultimate decided by the Ohio courts.

A recent legal challenge to home rule involved an incorporated city's authority to require their police officers to reside inside the city limits. This requirement was at odds with a recently enacted state statute that permitted non-city residents to serve as police officers. The Ohio supreme court finally settled this question. The trial court decision supported the plaintiff's effort to overturn the city's residency requirement, but an appellate court overturned the trial court's decision. In the end, Justice Paul Pfeifer, writing for the majority of the Ohio state supreme court, concluded that validly enacted state statutes "[prevailed] over conflicting local laws."[18]

The matter of home rule did find some supporters among the Ohio supreme court's dissenters. Justice Judith Lanzinger, for example, argued that "[q]ualifications regarding the residency of municipal employees are not aspects of police powers, but rather are matters of local self-government. Because this is not a matter of statewide concern, the ordinances should be upheld as a matter of self-governance."[19]

Special Districts

State law allows the creation of special districts in Ohio, governed by an appointed board. The U.S. Census Bureau reported that there were 700 such special districts in Ohio in 2012.[20] These districts usually have a single purpose and often have their own revenue source. This revenue source is usually a property tax; however, some county transit authorities are allowed to have a piggyback on the sales tax. Enabling statutes create and dictate the form of special districts in Ohio. For example, port authorities might be created by municipal ordinance or township or county resolution. A regional water and sewer district is created by order of the court of common pleas upon granting the petition of one or more political sub divisions.[21] The special districts can span part of a county or span a number of counties. A few examples of the types of special districts in Ohio include a county library district, a water district, a park district, a joint fire district, a sanitary district, a soil and water conservation district, a regional transit authority, a joint economic development district, or a regional airport authority. Frequently, these districts are created in response to a demand and a lack of mergers of local governments in Ohio municipal history.[22]

Public Records and Open Meetings

Ohio's public records and open meetings law provide citizens with the right to know what their state and local governments are doing. Public records are any forms, letters, or other written materials created or received by a unit of government. Electronic communications and records such as computer files, e-mails, and so on have come under the same statutes. These records are open to public inspection except for a few exemptions.

There is also an open meeting law in Ohio, called the *sunshine law,* that was passed in 1975. All meetings of any public body are declared to be public meetings open to the public at all times. Every meeting is subject to the sunshine law if (1) it is prearranged, (2) if it is attended by a majority of the members of the group involved, and (3) if public business is discussed. The sunshine law does permit closed meetings under certain specified conditions. The closed meetings are usually declared as executive sessions, where certain issues can be discussed behind closed doors, but no formal action is permitted. These exceptions include discussion of individual employees, the sale of property, discussions with an attorney, and preparation for collective bargaining. There was language inserted in the most recent budget bill that would allow Ohio local governments to go into executive session on issues concerning economic development. The Ohio Municipal League, taking its cue from the arguments for JobsOhio, requested this language. The Ohio Newspaper Association, however, objected to the new exception, arguing, "It is not hard to imagine circumstances that will lead to bad results with more secrecy involving the use of taxpayer dollars and special favors such as tax credits."[23]

Financing of Local Governments

The state of Ohio provides direct support to local governments through the local government fund (LGF), which is allocated to counties and then divided up among the various political subdivisions. The LGF has existed in Ohio since 1934, when the state passed a 3 percent sales tax for the purpose of supporting local government activities. In 1935, local governments received 40 percent of the monies generated by the sales tax and schools received the remaining 60 percent. As time went on, different revenue streams were added to this fund and two other funds were created.[24]

In his first year in office, Governor John Kasich was confronted with an $8 billion dollar shortfall for the fiscal year (FY) 2012–2013 budget. Kasich, in his efforts to cut state spending to balance the state budget for FY 2012 and FY 2013, placed the greatest burden on local governments by cutting the LGF by 25 percent in FY 2012 and 50 percent in FY 2013. In those budgets, the LGF amount was no longer expressed as a percentage of tax receipts (as had previously been the case) but as a fixed dollar amount. The FY 2014–2015 house budget, while incorporating the 50 percent cut into permanent law, went back to expressing the amount in terms of the percentage of tax receipts that would be dedicated to the LGF. There were other revenue losses imposed by the state on local governments and school districts. In 2005, House Bill 66 instituted a phaseout of the Tangible Personal Property Tax and the Public Utility Tangible Tax over a five-year period. The phaseout of these taxes further weakened the local government and school district's ability to collect revenue. In addition to that, under Governor Kasich, the Ohio inheritance tax in Ohio was phased out. Local governments had received a substantial share of that unpredictable revenue. In its most recent general fund budget, the state revoked the practice of the state paying the first 12.5 percent of newly adopted local property taxes. Over recent decades, Ohio's support for its local governments has been on the decline. The degree of state oversight and regulation has been on the increase.

Overall, the state defines the sources of revenue that Ohio local governments can collect as well as the requirements for the adoption of local taxes. As a result, voters have a great deal of control over local government taxes in Ohio. Townships are restricted to the use of property tax levies, which are frequently dedicated to specific purposes such as roads, police, and firefighters. The voters often must approve these levies.

The county government also provides a share of Ohio's local government funds to the townships. County governments in Ohio rely primarily on the piggyback tax, which is an add-on to the state sales tax. For example, the Montgomery County budget director said that sales tax revenues are 50 percent of that county's general fund revenues.[25] Piggyback sales tax increases are subject to a vote by the county citizens. The range for the county sales tax in Ohio is from .75 percent to 1.5 percent. The state collects the county sales tax and returns it to the counties.

Ohio's incorporated municipalities can impose an income tax. This tax was first imposed by the city of Toledo. The power of an incorporated municipality to impose an income tax has been upheld by the Ohio supreme court.[26] In 2009, 577 municipalities in Ohio levied an income tax, with rates ranging from 0.4 percent to 3 percent. Rates above 1 percent must be placed on the ballot for approval. Municipalities may offer partial or full credit to residents who pay municipal income taxes to a different municipality where they work. Most collections go into the general fund. Some part can be earmarked for capital improvement or the promise to use the funds for safety forces.[27] The tax is applied to wages of residents and nonresidents working in the municipality. It is also applied to net profits of business attributable to activities in the municipality. Administration of the collection of municipal income tax is the responsibility of the city or village imposing the tax. Recently, there was considerable contention between the municipalities and the state legislature when the state considered standardizing the municipal income tax, which was favored by Ohio certified public accountants and many business interests in Ohio. The issue continues to be considered by the Ohio general assembly

State Fiscal Oversight of Local Governments

The state of Ohio has oversight of the fiscal conditions of Ohio's cities, counties, and townships. The original municipal fiscal emergency legislation was enacted in 1979 in response to the fiscal crisis in Cleveland. At that time, the city of Cleveland was on the verge of bankruptcy. In 1996, fiscal emergency protection was extended to counties and townships. Then, in 2011, the legislature modified the procedure and added fiscal caution, a condition that could result in a declaration of fiscal watch or fiscal emergency.

The fiscal and budgetary condition that triggers the auditor to declare a municipal corporation, county, or township in *fiscal caution* occurs when the auditor deems that the financial records are not auditable. There are also financial triggers. An example of this is when a deficit fund at the end of the year is greater than 2 percent of that fund's revenue for the year. The auditor cannot release an entity from fiscal caution until the conditions that lead to the designation no longer exist.

More serious is when the state auditor places a local government in *fiscal watch*. A fiscal watch condition will be declared when "[a]ll accounts that were due and payable from the General Fund for more than 30 days, less the year-end balance of the General Fund, [exceed] one-twelfth of the General Fund budget for the year."[28] Once the auditor has declared a fiscal watch, the governing body has 120 days to submit a financial recovery plan. If this is not done in time, the auditor declares fiscal emergency conditions.

Since 1979, over 50 local governments have been declared to be in *fiscal emergency*. The conditions that lead to a declaration of fiscal emergency are similar to those for a fiscal watch but may also include the failure to meet payroll or debt obligations.[29] A local government entity declared to be in fiscal emergency comes under a state-imposed financial planning and supervision commission. The state auditor is the financial supervisor of the commission, which is made up of designated representatives of state offices, such as the treasurer of the state, the director of the Ohio Office of Budget and Management, officials of the local government, and three members appointed by the governor who are residents of the political subdivision and have at least five years of private sector business/financial experience.

The commission is to approve a financial recovery plan that will "eliminate the fiscal emergency conditions, balance the budget, avoid future deficits and market long-term obligations."[30] Most significantly,

> [t]he commission has widespread authority to review all revenue and expenditure estimates to determine whether they result in a balanced budget; require the government by ordinance or resolution to establish monthly levels of expenditures and encumbrances consistent with the financial plan; to approve and monitor these levels; to approve the amount and purpose of any debt issues; to make and enter into all contracts and agreements necessary to the performance of its duties and to make recommendations for cost reductions or revenue increases to carry out the financial plan.[31]

There are a number of additional conditions that the local government must meet to be released from fiscal emergency.[32] The state-appointed commission assumes most of the fiscal authority of the local government.

Conclusion

Ohio local governments, which include counties, townships, villages, and cities, are tightly governed by the state. The authority of political subdivisions to govern and raise revenue is limited by the state. Over the past decade, Ohio's financial support for local government has eroded while its oversight has increased. Recent Ohio supreme court decisions have supported this erosion of local government authority in Ohio.

Notes

1. Ohio Municipal League, *Municipal Government in Ohio 2012* (Columbus: 1992).
2. Ibid., 3.
3. Constitution of the State of Ohio (Annotated 1979), Article XVIII, Municipal Corporations 1 (Classifications).
4. Carl Broberg, *Local Government in Ohio* (Cincinnati: American Legal Publishing, 1995), 126–128.
5. The general assembly provides for three additional optional statutory forms. They include the commission form, the city manager form, and the federal plan.
6. Constitution of the State of Ohio.
7. Ohio Municipal League, *Municipal Government in Ohio 2012,* 20.
8. Ibid., 23.
9. See Note 2 above.
10. Ibid., 22.
11. "City of Dayton," accessed July 28, 2014, http://www.cityofdayton.org/Pages/default.aspx
12. Ohio Municipal League, *Municipal Government in Ohio 2012,* 14.
13. Ibid.
14. Carl Broberg, *Local Government in Ohio* (Cincinnati: American Legal Publishing, 1995), 108.
15. Constitution of the State of Ohio (Annotated 1979), Article X, Sections 3, 4.
16. "What You Should Know about Annexation," Ohio State Bar Association, accessed October 23, 2014, https://www.ohiobar.org/ForPublic/Resources/LawYouCanUse/Pages/LawYouCanUse-463.aspx
17. Sam Hendren, "How Annexation Works in Columbus," *WOSU Public Media,* June 5, 2011.
18. Lima v. State, 122 Ohio St.3rd 155, 2009-Ohio-2598.
19. Ibid.
20. "Lists & Structure of Governments," United States Census Bureau, accessed October 23, 2014, http://www.census.gov/govs/go/special_district_governments.html
21. Cleveland-Marshall College of Law Library, "Forms of Government," Ohio Local Government Law Resource Guide, accessed October 21, 2014, http://guides.law.csuohio.edu/content.php?pid=412696&sid=3371630

22. League of Women Voters of Ohio, *Know Your Ohio Government*, 7th ed. (Columbus: Author, 1993).
23. Randy Ludlow, "Bill Would Allow Secret Meetings on Economic Development," *Columbus Dispatch*, June 7, 2013, accessed October 21, 2014, http://www.dispatch.com/content/blogs/your-right-to-know/2013/06/development.html
24. "Ohio's Local Government Funds," accessed October 21, 2014, http://www.olc.org/pdf/OHLocalGovernmentsCCAO.pdf
25. Chelsey Levingston, "Sales Taxes a Bright Spot for County Government Revenues," *Dayton Daily News*, May 29, 2013.
26. Ohio Municipal League, *Municipal Government in Ohio 2012*, 155.
27. "Municipal Income Taxes," Department of Taxation, accessed October 21, 2014, http://www.tax.ohio.gov/municipalities/municipal_income_tax_forms.aspx
28. "Local Governments & Fiscal Distress," Dave Yost, Ohio Auditor, accessed July 27, 2014, https://ohioauditor.gov/fiscal/local.html
29. Ibid.
30. Ibid.
31. Ibid.
32. Ibid.

CHAPTER 7

Financing the State Government of Ohio

The Ohio Budget

Budgeting is one of the most important functions of state government, and that is certainly true in Ohio. The state budget of Ohio is much more than a financial spreadsheet; it is a policy document. Any change in spending by either increasing funds for some agencies or cutting funds for others creates a change in the policy outcome. The state budget is therefore also a statement of policy priorities. In Ohio, K–12 education funding takes the largest share of state-owned revenue, and the spending and distribution of those funds is always a matter of contention. There are a number of characteristics of the Ohio budget that are notable. First, although the general revenue fund (GRF) budget is a biennial (two-year) budget, each year's budget is a separate appropriation. Second, the GRF budget must end in balance in each of the two fiscal years. Ohio's fiscal year (FY) begins on July 1 of the prior year and ends on June 30. This means that FY 2014 actually began in July of 2013 and ended in June of 2014. Finally, the state government in Ohio passes a mid-biennium correction budget. This was once used merely to make minor corrections to the budget based on more up-to-date revenue and spending data. Under Governor John Kasich, this has come to be known as the mid-biennium budget review (MBR) and is now a vehicle to make much larger changes to Ohio law.

Ohio has a number of other budgets in addition to the GRF budget. There is a separate transportation budget, done in the same year as the GRF budget, and also a capital budget, which is usually completed in non-GRF budget years.

Ohio's Revenue Sources

As Figure 7.1 shows, Ohio relies on the state's individual income tax, the state's sales tax, and significant federal grants and reimbursements to fund Ohio

FIGURE 7.1 GRF Revenues by Source

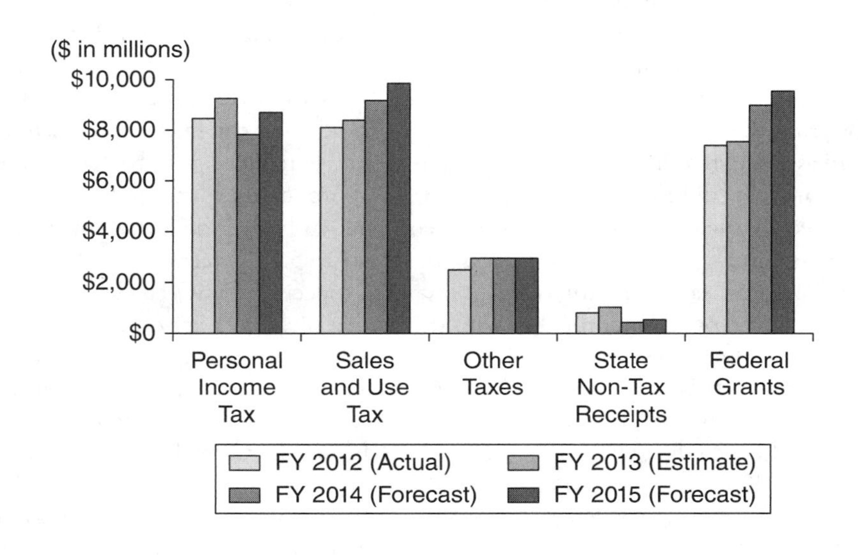

Source: "Budget in Brief," Ohio Legislative Service Commission, accessed October 19, 2014, http://www.lsc.state.oh.us/fiscal/budgetinbrief130/budgetinbrief-hb59-in.pdf

government. These federal monies are primarily matching Medicaid funds. The most recent data show that the federal share (FMAP) of Ohio's Medicaid expenditures totals 63 percent. Of course, that percentage is likely to grow as the Affordable Care Act's (ACA) Medicaid expansion goes into effect in Ohio. Under the ACA, the federal government will pay 100 percent of the cost of that expansion for the first three years.

Ohio Sales and Use Tax

Current budget estimates are that the Ohio sales tax (formally called the *sales and use tax*) will surpass all other state revenue sources in the GRF. The sales tax was enacted in 1934 by the general assembly and initially set at the rate of 3 percent. In 1967, this rate was raised to 4 percent. In 1981, it was again raised, this time to 5.1 percent. In response to complaints by vendors, however, it was quickly reduced to 5 percent but broadened to include cigarettes. In the early 1990s, the Ohio legislature expanded the tax base even more, including for the first time a number of services such as cleaning and maintenance work. There was an effort by Governor George Voinovich in 1998 to raise it by 1 percent and have the added revenue dedicated to education in order to address the seemingly endless legal battle in Ohio over school funding. The measure was placed on the ballot as an initiative but was defeated. In 2003, the tax was temporarily raised to 6 percent before being lowered to 5.5 percent in 2005.

Governor Kasich, in his second biennial budget (FY 2014–2015), proposed lowering the sales tax rate to 5 percent and broadening the sales tax to include some services that had not previously been taxed. He received push back from the legislature, as did previous Ohio governors who proposed expanding the services covered by the sales tax.[1] The most recent biennial budget deliberations ended with an actual quarter-percent increase in the tax to 5.75 percent.

The sales tax on motor vehicle purchases, especially light vehicle sales, is a major source of revenue for the state. If motor vehicle sales are down, the state sales tax receipts fall significantly. This points to the major problem with financing government through a sales tax: Sales tax revenue is very elastic, and a downturn in the economy will result in significant revenue reductions. This fact compounded the budget challenges facing Ohio during the Great Recession, which began in 2008.

One increasing challenge for the collection of state sales tax in Ohio, as in other states that rely on a sales tax, is the problem of collecting the tax on purchases conducted on the Internet. Amazon, one of the nation's largest online retailers, reports that it collects sales tax for sixteen states. Ohio is not one of them. Technically, Ohioans who make purchases over the Internet are required to pay the sales tax. Unless the company has a physical presence in Ohio, however, the company is not required to collect that tax at the point of sale. Although some companies voluntarily collect the tax, many do not. There was an attempt to address this in the Ohio house version of the FY 2014–2015 budget. Governor Kasich, however, said that he preferred for the federal government to resolve this tax issue. The issue has yet to be resolved at the federal level.

Ohio State Income Tax

The second most significant nonfederal source of GRF revenue for Ohio is the state's individual income tax. The Ohio income tax had its origins in a 1912 constitutional amendment permitting the taxation of income in Ohio. However, the income tax was not made law in Ohio until 1971. It was enacted under the leadership of Democratic Governor John Gilligan and a Republican-controlled general assembly. Governor Gilligan was subsequently defeated in his bid for reelection in 1974. One of the major reasons for his defeat was the adoption of the state income tax.

Raising the income tax is considered an anathema to Ohio politicians. The Ohio income tax rate is considered progressive insofar as taxes for higher incomes are at higher rates. The top rate, applied to incomes over $204,200, was 5.92 percent. Governor Kasich, in his 2014 mid-biennium budget, proposed dropping the top rate below 5 percent, with a corresponding increase to the severance tax (explained below) on the natural gas fracking industry. The legislature agreed instead to reduce the top rate to 5.3 percent and limiting that rate to income over $208,500 per year.

Severance Taxes

One of the taxes that has received little attention but that Governor Kasich has an affinity for is the severance tax. A severance tax is a tax on nonrenewable resources extracted from the earth. The severance tax imposed in Ohio has never been a very significant revenue generator. In 2011, for example, the severance tax generated $11.2 million.[2] This is an insignificant sum in Ohio's budget. Governor Kasich, however, has promoted the idea of increasing the severance tax because of the expected boom in natural gas and oil production resulting from the forecasted expansion of fracking in Ohio. The governor argues that the severance tax will yield a bonanza of revenues for the state and can be used to lower taxes for ordinary Ohio taxpayers. So far, however, he has been unsuccessful in persuading the legislature to increase this tax.

State Non-Tax Receipts

State non-tax receipts include the proceeds of fines and forfeitures and the sale of goods and services as well as receipts from local governments. Earnings on investments made by the treasurer of state also go into the Ohio GRF.[3] Proceeds from the Division of Liquor Control, which once went into the GRF, are now transferred to JobsOhio.[4]

Federal Grants

Figure 7.1 showed that federal grants were projected to be the second-largest revenue source for the state of Ohio in FY 2014 and FY 2015. This is based on estimates contained in the budget passed by the legislature in 2013 that does not include the Medicaid monies that were eventually accepted by action of the Controlling Board in the fall of 2013. Medicaid makes up the lion's share of Ohio's federal grant money. Those new Medicaid monies will very likely make federal grants the largest revenue source for the state of Ohio.

Federal funds transferred to Ohio are called *intergovernmental transfers*. Those federal funds are frequently divided into two categories: categorical grants and block grants. Categorical grants contain specific requirements and conditions.

Since most of the federal aid coming to Ohio from the federal government is Medicaid and there are many strings attached, most federal aid to Ohio is in the form of categorical grants. The other type of federal grant is called a block grant, where the recipient government (in this case, the state of Ohio) has significant latitude in the spending of the federal money. When it was passed under the Clinton administration, Temporary Assistance to Needy Families (TANF) was termed a block grant. The state would determine the benefit and provide some of the matching money for the program. It is difficult, however, to draw a sharp line between categorical grants and block grants. TANF may be a very good example of this confusion, since when Governor Kasich began to more strictly enforce the work requirements for recipients of TANF money, he claimed that it was required by the federal government.[5] That raises some doubt about the degree of latitude granted to the state by what the federal government calls a block grant. In this case, it appears the state policy is directed by federal rules.

Property Tax

Property tax is governed by Ohio law but is not included in Figure 7.1 because it is not a revenue source for state government in Ohio. Instead, as explained in Chapter 6, property tax revenue in Ohio goes directly to local and township governments, school districts, and other special districts. For townships, it is their only permitted means for generating revenue. State law governs the use and imposition of the property tax. In Ohio, the property tax is applied to the taxable value of land and buildings. The base upon which it is assessed is 35 percent of the market value of property. Ohio property tax rates are expressed in terms of millage. One "mill" is .001 percent, or one-tenth of 1 percent of assessed value. So if a home is valued at $100,000, it is taxed at a value of $35,000. One mill would therefore generate $35 ($35,000 × .001).

The Ohio constitution prohibits taxes on property that exceed 1 percent of the true or market value of the property without voter approval in the taxing district.[6] Statutes clarify that the language means that ten mills of un-voted property tax can be levied against taxable property. Property taxes levied within the ten mills are often called *inside millage*, because it is within the constitutional limit. Additional millage, which must be approved by voters, is called *outside millage*.[7]

In the mid-1970s, due to a high rate of inflation, there were significant increases in the value of real property in the United States. Increases in property taxes reflected that increase in value. Voters in California reacted to this by voting for Proposition 13, which restricted the growth in property taxes. The Ohio legislature addressed this increasing property tax issue by adopting House Bill 920 in 1976. House Bill 920 froze locally approved levies at the value of the residential property at the time the levy was approved.[8] Future increases in assessed value will not generate additional revenue, with the exception of new construction within the political subdivision. This has been a challenge for Ohio school districts and townships, which rely on property taxes for revenue. Every six years, the county auditor must reassess the value of property in the county, but increases in the value will not bring about increased revenue from the existing levies.

The state of Ohio offers property tax relief to various populations. The most recent was the expansion of what is known as the *Homestead Exemption*. This exemption shields up to $25,000 of the market value of a home from taxation. The state makes up the lost revenue to the affected school districts and political subdivisions. In 2007, under Democratic Governor Ted Strickland, the Homestead Exemption was expanded to include, regardless of income, all those defined as permanently disabled and seniors 65 years of age and over. The Ohio chamber of commerce successfully proposed returning to a means-tested homestead exemption for seniors in the FY 2014–2015 biennial budget. Homeowners over 65 will now have to meet certain income guidelines to enjoy this tax relief.

In addition to changing the Homestead Exemption, the state has withdrawn the subsidy for the first 12.5 percent of new property tax levies. Prior to this change in law, the state paid the first 12.5 percent of the property tax for voted levies.

The Budget Process in Ohio

There is no constitutional or statutory requirement for Ohio to use a biennial budget, and in fact, Ohio is the largest public entity in the United States to use a two-year budget cycle.[9] There are some merits to a biennial budget, and occasionally, that budgeting approach is recommended for the federal government's budget process. The benefit is that it reduces the annual political conflict over budget making and reduces uncertainty of annual budgets. The obvious downside is the challenge of making a 24-month economic forecast for a budget that must be in balance at the end of each of the two fiscal years.

The process of preparing the GFR budget begins with a call by the Ohio Office of Budget and Management (OBM) to the state agencies and departments asking them to submit their requests for the next FY. For FY 2014–2015, the agencies were asked to "describe what activities can be supported at 90% of adjusted fiscal year 2013 appropriations for fiscal years 2014 and 2015."[10] They were also asked to submit a listing of activities that could be supported at 100 percent of the 2013 FY budget. These requests had to be in by October 1, 2012, since FY 2014 would actually commence on July 1, 2013.

After the agency requests are submitted, the OBM develops the executive budget that must be presented by the governor to the legislature four weeks after the beginning of each general assembly. That deadline is delayed until March 15 for a newly elected governor. A number of department and agency spending projections are complicated by, for example, the uncertainty of projected caseloads for entitlement programs such as Medicaid and student enrollment numbers in schools and universities.

In the development of the executive budget, one of the critical challenges for OBM is forecasting revenue over the course of two years. Since the budget must be in balance each year (the state can incur $750,000 of debt, a paltry sum in a multibillion-dollar state budget) that revenue forecast determines the level of spending. OBM's task of projecting the state's revenue is complicated by the fact that estimates are predicted on the performance of the state's economy. Of course, sales and income taxes vary with the business cycle. These revenue constraints can be relieved by tax increases, which in recent decades is seen by many as a fatal political move in Ohio politics. The OBM is not the only government agency making revenue projections. The Ohio Legislative Services Commission (LSC) also produces revenue forecasts. In 2013, the Ohio house relied on the LSC for its revenue forecast during its FY 2014–2015 GRF budget debates, since the LSC's numbers were slightly more optimistic than OBM's prediction.[11]

If monies collected over a FY exceed the amount appropriated, the governor can carry them over into a rainy day fund. This is a frequent source of executive-legislative friction, because the legislature prefers to spend this money. Nevertheless, Governor Kasich took great pride in the fact that he was able to expand the rainy day fund from being nearly broke to having a surplus of 1.5 billion dollars. If the revenues do not meet the forecasted annual revenues and there is an imbalance, the Ohio governor has the authority to impose a recession (cuts) in state spending to ensure that there is a balanced budget at the end of each FY (June 30).

The executive budget is presented to the legislature, which has until the end of June to enact the budget. After the governor submits the executive budget to the legislature, the LSC puts it in a form of a bill. The bill then goes to the Ohio house Rules and Reference Committee, which assigns it to the house Finance and Appropriations Committee. For the FY 2014–2015 budget, Speaker William Batchelder decided that there would be five house Finance and Appropriation subcommittees. The subcommittees were Agriculture and Development, Higher Education, Primary and Secondary Education, Transportation, and Health and Human Services. This was not a new or unique division of subcommittees.

The various house subcommittees hold hearings and take testimony from proponents and opponents of the executive budget, which serves as the working budget document of the general assembly. Representatives of state agencies and interest groups testify before these subcommittees regarding the executive request. The agency heads offer the initial testimony, and it is expected that they will support the executive budget and not make an end run around the governor by seeking more money directly from the legislature. Although committee members might ask questions of those testifying, there is very little public deliberation. Instead, most of the decisions are made and the final outline of the house budget bill is determined in the majority party caucus. Governors, even when they share an affiliation with the majority party caucus, cannot depend on their budget recommendations being accepted. In preparing the house FY 2014–2015 GRF budget bill, house Republicans rejected many of Governor Kasich's recommendations for spending and taxes. The governor had proposed expanding the sales tax to services such as legal fees while lowering the sales tax rate. He also proposed lowering the income tax by 20 percent and imposing a severance tax on the emerging Ohio fracking industry. On the spending side, the governor wanted to expand Medicaid to cover everyone in Ohio at or below 18 percent of the federal poverty level. The federal government would pay 100 percent of the cost for the first few years under the ACA. Almost all of Kasich's proposals were altered or were turned down by the Republican-controlled Ohio house when they sent their substitute budget bill to the senate in mid-April of 2013.

The house substitute budget bill goes to the senate Finance Committee. In a similar pattern to that found in the Ohio house of representatives, the senate Finance Committee then sends the bill to subcommittees to hold hearings. After the hearings, the senate votes on its own amended version of the budget bill. The GRF budget bill that came out of the senate in 2013 was 5,371 pages in length. That total was 1,160 pages longer than Governor Kasich's initial budget document.

Conference Committee

There are frequently differences between the house and senate versions of the budget bill. The conference committee addresses these differences. The conference committee is composed of members of both houses, and its job is to resolve their differences. The committee is supposed to focus only on the differences in the bills offered by each legislative body. This is, however, not always the case. In 2013, for example, the conference committee on the budget did more than resolve differences. The committee adopted a new policy. In that year, the house formally rejected the senate version of the budget, which is required to trigger a conference committee. The conference committee was then made up of six members, three from the house and three from the senate. Each of these three-member groups contained two Republicans and one Democrat.

Conference committee deliberations are held behind closed doors. Greg Lawson, policy analyst of the conservative Buckeye Institute, described the process as one where "[p]eople will come and testify, but like the whole process, there is a lot that happens during internal conversations."[12] In 2013, OBM Director Tim Keen, as expected, gave testimony to the conference committee. One reason this is done is to take into account the latest revenue estimates for the final budget bill, and in that year, the house and senate versions of the bill had higher baseline estimates than the executive budget. Keen advised the conference committee "to be conservative in the adoption of both revenue and Medicaid estimates."[13] This somewhat pessimistic approach is typical of executive branch budget makers. They tend to be cautious in their estimates and prefer a surplus to deficits, because if economy falters and revenues do not meet forecasts, the burden of cuts rests with the governor.

Both chambers of the Ohio general assembly must vote on the eventual conference committee report in the form of a budget bill. If it passes, the bill goes on to the governor for his or her signature. Budget bills are different from other passed legislation in Ohio in that they are subject to the line item veto. Normally, governors must veto entire bills, but the Ohio constitution says that "the governor may disapprove any item or items in any bill making an appropriation of money."[14] The Ohio supreme court has expanded this to allow governors to line item veto a provision of substantive law that is included in appropriations bills.[15] Like a regular veto, a line item veto can be overridden by a three-fifths vote in each chamber.

In 2013, Governor Kasich exercised his line item veto power to veto 22 items in the massive two-year state budget. In his remarks explaining his vetoes, the governor highlighted cutting language that blocked him from moving forward with Medicaid expansion.

The Mid-Biennium Budget Review (MBR)

Governor Kasich has significantly expanded the scope of what was once called the *corrections budget bill*. It is a bill designed to correct defects and oversights in the biennial budget in the middle year of the biennium. The bill is now called the MBR. In 2014, Governor Kasich proposed an expansive MBR with significant policy proposals. The MBR was so large, the house broke the proposed executive MBR into a number of separate bills that were eventually passed by both houses and signed by the governor.

The MBR bills, when passed, included a variety of other nonfinancial items, such as allowing craft beer pubs that have breweries on a separate site to sell growlers of beer. It also permitted a drug counselor to earn a "gambling disorder" endorsement on his or her license and required districts to create parental advisory committees to review textbooks and curriculum. One can see that the MBR is now far removed from its origins as a limited budget corrections budget bill.

Expenditures: Where State Funds Go in Ohio

State expenditures in Ohio can be grouped into five items: K–12 education, health and human services, higher education, corrections, and general government expenses. Figure 7.2 displays these expenditures for FY 2012. The amounts listed for FY 2013, 2014, and 2015 are projections. The sums include federal grant monies but do not include the additional Medicaid funds from the expansion of that program.

This omission may be significant, since the federal funds included in these expenditure numbers budget, especially Medicaid, significantly boosts the human services line. If the spending of federal funds were not included, K–12 education would account for 39.5 percent of all spending, slightly higher than human services (which would be at 32.9 percent). That means that most of Ohio's own revenues are spent on K–12 education. Note that funding for higher education in Ohio (state universities and community colleges) is relatively flat over the displayed years. Of course, higher education institutions can seek additional revenue by raising tuition, but in recent years, the legislature has capped tuition increases for higher education at a relatively low percentage. The corrections budget also shows little increase over the budget years displayed in Figure 7.2. In recent decades, Ohio has privatized and, in some instances, sold its prisons to private corporations to operate.

FIGURE 7.2 Total (State and Federal) GRF Appropriations

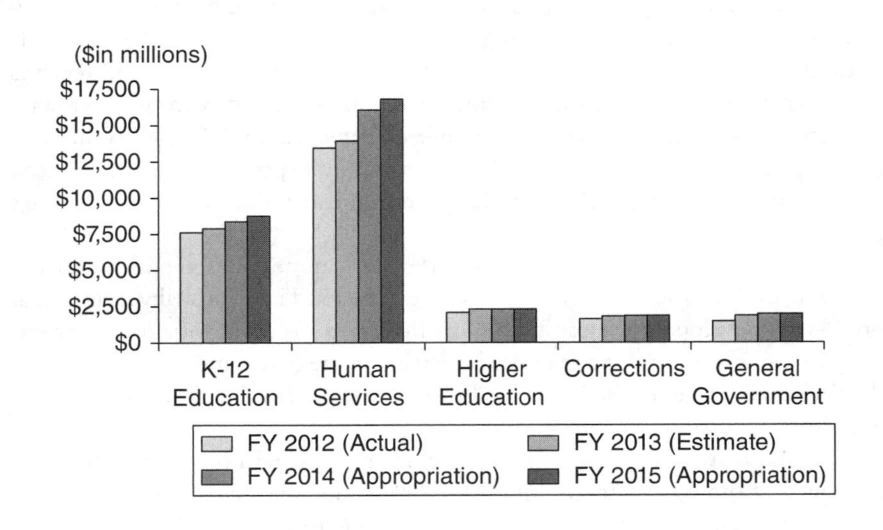

Source: "Budget in Brief," Ohio Legislative Service Commission, http://www.lsc.state.oh.us/fiscal/budgetinbrief130/budgetinbrief-hb59-in.pdf

Executive Budget Cutting

The Ohio budget is kept in balance because, if the revenue forecast has been too rosy for a fiscal year, the legislature has granted the executive the authority to cut appropriated funds to achieve a balanced budget.[16] The constitutionality of this grant of authority has never been directly tested in court. Governor Voinovich went so far in exercising this power that instead of instituting across-the-board cuts, he made selective cuts of up to 50 percent for certain agencies and exempted other agencies from any cuts. These cuts are often called a *rescission.*

The Capital Budget

Ohio has a separate capital budget. The state's capital budget funds the acquisition or construction of major capital items in Ohio, including land purchases, building construction, and equipment. The capital budget is biennial but is developed and enacted in the year opposite the adoption of the GFR biennial state budget.

The sale of bonds is considered to be the most prudent way to pay for these large capital projects. There are two types of bonds that the state can issue. The first are *general obligation bonds,* which are backed by the full faith and credit of the state. The second type is known as a *revenue bond,* where some particular revenue stream generated by the project will pay off the debt.[17] The more common type of bond issued by Ohio is the revenue bond. A revenue bond can be issued in Ohio for "capital improvements for mental illness and retardation, parks and recreation and institutions of higher education."[18] Purchasers of these bonds not only have claim on the revenue generated by the project but on all receipts generated by those state entities. Ohio makes appropriations from other state funds to support capital projects. A notable example was in 2000, when the state of Ohio set aside part of the $25 billion the state expected from the tobacco settlement to support a local matching program to build and rebuild Ohio's public schools.

The capital budget process begins in the late summer of each odd-numbered year, when OBM distributes guidelines to the agencies. There is usually an informal process for developing the capital budget involving closed negotiations between the governor's office and the majority leadership in the house and the senate. Once the leadership agrees to the items on the list, the capital budget bill usually passes with little discussion.

Capital budgets in Ohio generally include projects resulting from a wish list of requests from cities and communities throughout the state. This community project list includes everything from art museums to sports facilities. Although these projects usually have strong local support, to outsiders, they can seem like "pork-barrel" spending.

The FY 2015–2016 capital appropriation for Ohio totaled $2.4 billion. The largest fund, $675 million, was for the School Building Assistance Program. Governor Voinovich initiated this state support for school construction in response to the Ohio supreme court decisions declaring Ohio's school funding scheme to be in violation of the Ohio constitution (a ruling that has never been fully complied with by the state legislature). This program is used to assist school districts in constructing or refurbishing school buildings. Of that amount, $100 million is to come from licensing fees paid by racetracks for electronic slot machines. In order to access this state support, a local school district is required to provide matching funds, which often requires a voted school levy.

FY 2015–2016 was the first biennial capital budget in six years to include funding for community projects. The total amount, $160 million, included monies for the improvement of art museums and theatres throughout the state as well as $10 million for the Pro Football Hall of Fame in Canton and $1 million for the Rock and Roll Hall of Fame in Cleveland.

The capital budget can only appropriate money for two years. If the money is not spent during the biennium, it requires reappropriation. The FY 2015–2016 capital budget bill ultimately included money for projects that had not been spent in FY 2013–2014. The reappropriated capital funds totaled $1.64 billion and were in the same bill as the new capital appropriations.

The Transportation Budget

Although it is done in the same year, the transportation budget, which is also a biennial budget, is separate from the GRF budget. The transportation budget for FY 2014–2015 totaled $7.6 billion (see Table 7.1). The source of funds for Ohio transportation projects and Ohio Department of Transportation (ODOT) operations is the state Motor Fuel Tax (MFT). The current MFT rate is 28 cents per gallon of gasoline. These revenues are dedicated to transportation and are often used as a match for federal funds. Because of more fuel-efficient vehicles and the impact of the recession, revenues from the MFT have been flat over recent years. This is reflected in Figure 7.3. Reliance on a fixed tax expressed in cents is a growing problem for Ohio and other states. The revenues are not keeping pace with their transportation needs.

As discussed in Chapter 4, Governor Kasich has accessed Ohio Turnpike toll revenue to fund some of the state's highway projects. Of these turnpike funds, the latest transportation budget bill appropriated $200 million in FY 2014 and $300 million in FY 2015. Because the turnpike runs only through northern Ohio, these turnpike-revenue-generated funds were restricted by statute to projects north of U.S. Route 30. The focus of Ohio's transportation funds is highway

FIGURE 7.3 Motor Fuel Tax: Motor Fuel Tax Receipts versus Gallons Taxed

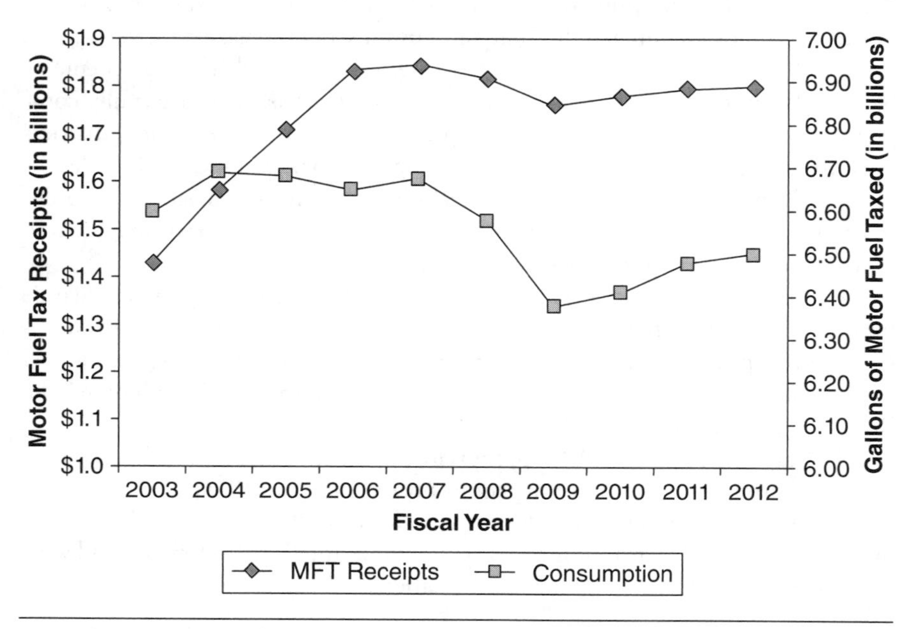

Source: "LSC Redbook: Analysis of the Executive Budget Proposal: Transportation Budget Bill (H. B. 35 of the 130th General Assembly)," Ohio Legislative Service Commission, http://www.lsc.state.oh.us/fiscal/transportation/transbudget130/trans-redbook-with-attachments.pdf

construction and maintenance. In comparison, very little is spent on other forms of transportation in Ohio.

Budget Execution

After the general assembly has appropriated monies and the governor has signed the budget bills, the budget bill as described above (passed and signed) is a grant of spending authority. It is not money to the respective agency. This is done through the OBM and the Controlling Board. The OBM is responsible for keeping all necessary accounting records and reconciling differences between the amounts appropriated and the aggregate totals. The OBM evaluates and recommends improvements to the internal controls used by state agencies. The OBM also issues the official comprehensive annual financial report of the state. The OBM has extensive accounting responsibilities. The Controlling Board is discussed below.

TABLE 7.1 Transportation Budget (in millions)

Functional category	*FY 2014*	*FY 2015*	*Biennium Total*	*% of total budget*
Highway transportation	$2,776.2	$2,911.2	$5,687.4	92.8%
Administration	$91.2	$92.5	$183.7	3.0%
Public transportation	$53.8	$53.8	$107.6	1.8%
Planning and research	$50.0	$50.7	$100.7	1.6%
Rail transportation	$17.0	$17.0	$34.0	0.6%
Aviation	$6.9	$7.0	$13.9	0.2%
Total	$2,995.2	$3,132.2	$6,127.4	100.0%

Source: "LSC Redbook: Analysis of the Executive Budget Proposal: Transportation Budget Bill (H.B. 35 of the 130th General Assembly)," Ohio Legislative Service Commission, http://www.lsc.state.oh.us/fiscal/transportation/transbudget130/trans-redbook-with-attachments.pdf

The Controlling Board

The Ohio State Controlling Board was created in 1917, and until 1969, it consisted of the governor, the attorney general, the auditor, and the chairpersons of the Ohio house and senate Finance Committees. It was intended to serve as an interim body to make minor budget changes and issue waivers to the competitive bidding process. The current form of the board was created in 1969. It is presided over by an appointee of the OBM and has six legislative members, two of whom by statute are the chairs of the house and senate Finance Committees. The remaining members are appointees of the legislative leadership (with two from each house), including one member from each of the major political parties. The Controlling Board is a unique institution in that it has both executive and legislative powers.

The Controlling Board meets regularly, usually every other Monday, and the meetings are public. Most items before the board are approved as a block, with a few more controversial items held for discussion. Ohio Democratic Party Chair Chris Redfern, who was also a member of the Ohio house, served as the house minority member on the Controlling Board and used that platform to criticize state Republican office holders.

The Controlling Board has extensive power under the Ohio law. The board can

1. transfer funds within an agency or move money appropriated to one agency into another agency's budget,

2. authorize the expenditure of capital appropriations for purposes other than originally provided for in the capital appropriations act (however, when doing this, the board can not authorize the use for these funds for operation purposes),
3. alter the requirements for advertisement for bids for construction, repair, or other improvements of any building, and
4. waive competitive bidding requirements for specified types of contracts. The Controlling Board has authority over leases that exceed a certain amount.[19]

Perhaps the most important aspect is that no money can be released for capital construction projects without the approval of the Controlling Board.

In 2013, Governor Kasich was able to use the Controlling Board to essentially bypass the legislature and take advantage of the ACA's Medicaid expansion. Although this act was challenged, the supreme court eventually upheld the board's actions.

BOX 7.1: The Controlling Board Expands Medicaid in Ohio

In the fall of 2013, after months of a disagreement between the Republican governor John Kasich and the Republican general assembly over the expansion of Medicaid, the governor took his last remaining option before pressing for a ballot initiative: He asked the Ohio Controlling Board to approve the proposed federal Medicaid expansion. On October 21, 2013, the Controlling Board panel approved spending $2.56 billion in federal money to expand Medicaid insurance coverage to an estimated 275,000 Ohioans. The vote made Ohio the 25th state to adopt the Medicaid expansion under the federal Affordable Care Act. The vote was 5 to 2. Randy Cole, the chair of the Controlling Board and the governor's representative, voted yes, as did the two Democratic members. At the last hour, the Speaker of the house and the president of the senate replaced members on the Controlling Board and the Medicaid expansion was adopted.

The following day, the Ohio-based 1851 Center for Constitutional Law filed a suit with the Ohio supreme court on behalf of six members of the Ohio house of representatives. The suit contended that the Controlling Board exceeded its authority when it voted to expand Medicaid. The Ohio supreme court agreed to an expedited hearing on this matter, and in December of 2013, by a vote of 4 to 3, agreed to uphold the action of the Controlling Board and stated that the Controlling Board had the authority to accept and spend the federal Medicaid funds. For the court, the relevant statutory provision provided that "[t]he Controlling Board shall take no action which does not carry out the legislative intent of the general assembly regarding program goals and levels of support of state agencies as expressed in the prevailing act of the general assembly."[1] In this case, although the legislature had enacted language restricting the governor from spending money on Medicaid expansion, that language had been vetoed, and there had been no effort to override the veto.

Note

1. Ohio Revised Code 127.17, accessed October 25, 2014, Codes.ohio.gov/orc/127.17

Conclusion

State finances need the attention of Ohio citizens. A budget is not a mere recording of revenues and expenditures. There are significant policy decisions embedded in a state budget. For example, in the latest Ohio budget, the state moved from a progressive tax structure to a more regressive tax structure by putting greater weight on the sales tax for its major revenue source. This policy decision has other implications because consumers are increasingly making purchases online, which frequently means that these purchases avoid the Ohio sales tax.

A point worth noting is that even though Ohio has the initiative to propose constitutional amendments (see Chapter 9), this power has not been used to restrict the discretion of the legislature on budget matters. This is in stark contrast to states such as California, where the initiative has been used to alter the budgeting process and mandate specific spending for specific programs. There have been similar budget proposals placed on the ballot in Ohio, but the voters have, so far, not approved any of them.

Notes

1. "Kasich Budget Would Cut Income Taxes across the Board, Raise Revenues Elsewhere; Medicaid Shake-Up Planned" *Gongwer Ohio* Vol. #82, Report 22, Article 1, February 1, 2013.
2. Ibid., 72.
3. Richard Sheridan, *Follow the Money: Ohio State Budgeting* (Cleveland: Federation for Community Planning, 2000), 50.
4. Ohio Revised Code, Section 4313.
5. Catherine Candisky, "More Ohioans Sign Up for Welfare," *Columbus Dispatch*, November 25, 2013.
6. Ohio constitution, Article XII, Section 2.

7. Sheridan, *Follow the Money*, 15.
8. Ibid., 28.
9. Ibid., 20.
10. Ohio OBM Operating Budget Guidance: 2014-2015.8.
11. Ohio Legislative Service Commission, "Baseline Forecast of GRF Revenues and Medicaid Expenditures for the FY 2014–2015 Biennial Budget," *Testimony Before the House Finance and Appropriations Committee,* February 5, 2013, accessed October 19, 2014, http://www.lsc.state.oh.us/fiscal/revenueforecasts/forecasts130/house-finance-testimony.pdf
12. Brandon Blackwell, "Experts Say Final Work on Ohio's Budget Will Happen Mostly Behind Closed Doors," *Plain Dealer*, June 15, 2013, accessed October 19, 2014, http://www.cleveland.com/open/index.ssf/2013/06/post_47.html
13. Ibid., 14.
14. Ohio constitution, Article II, Section 16.
15. Ibid.
16. Ohio Revised Code, Section 126.08.
17. Sheridan, *Follow the Money*, 199.
18. Ibid., 199.
19. Ibid., 126.

CHAPTER 8

Political Parties, Interest Groups, and Elections in Ohio

Major and Minor Parties in Ohio

Ohio has a very rich history of strong political parties. The Ohio Democratic Party is older than the Republican Party, having its origins in the founding period of the state. Initially, a party known as the Federalists served as the main rival to the Democratic Party (or the Democratic or Jeffersonian Republicans, as they were sometimes known). As the Federalist Party faded, the Whig Party emerged as the opponent of the Democrats.[1] The Whigs were strong in the "Western Reserve" part of the state, which is the northeast corner of Ohio. The Whig Party held to strong abolitionist views and so served as the natural core for the emergence of Republican Party in Ohio in the 1850s.

Beyond the Democrats and the Republicans, minor political parties have struggled to gain ballot access and sustain their legal status in Ohio. In the 2012 general election, no minor parties received even 1 percent of the vote, although the Libertarian Party presidential candidate came close, receiving .89 percent of the popular vote. Among the other minor parties, the Socialist Party presidential candidate received .05 percent of the vote, while the Constitution Party received .15 percent and the Green Party received .33 percent.

Even though third parties do not currently have much hope for winning the plurality of the vote necessary to actually be awarded an office in Ohio, they can affect a close election by siphoning off votes that might otherwise go to one of the major party candidates. For this reason, it is sometimes said that there is only one thing Ohio Republicans and Democrats agree on: making it difficult for third parties to gain ballot access.

Prior to 2006, Ohio law required minor political parties to collect signatures equivalent to 1 percent of the total vote cast in the most recent statewide election in order to have their candidate's name placed on the ballot. These signatures had to be submitted at least 120 days prior to the primary election. Once they appeared on the ballot, the minor party's gubernatorial candidate (or slate of electors in a presidential year) had to attract at least 5 percent of the total votes cast. If the party failed to cross the 5 percent threshold, they had to start all over again.

In response to a legal challenge brought by the Libertarian Party of Ohio, a federal court declared those requirements unconstitutional in 2006.[2] The Ohio legislature did not alleviate the legal problems with the statute, and when the secretary of state of Ohio attempted to step into the breach, a second federal court declared her actions to be unconstitutional. The result was that it became fairly easy for minor parties to go to court to seek access to the Ohio ballot. These minor parties were allowed to have ballot access even if they did not meet the 5 percent threshold. Prior to this court ruling, Ohio rarely had more than one minor political party on the ballot in any election. In the period from 2006 until 2013, the Green Party, the Libertarian Party, Constitution Party, the Socialist Party, and the American Election Party all gained access to Ohio's ballot. Ohio also established that if two or more candidates filed for the nomination for the same office of the same minor party, the state would conduct a primary election.[3]

In November of 2013, the Republican-controlled general assembly passed a new ballot access measure for minor political parties. The new law requires minor parties to collect one-half of 1 percent of the vote cast in the last presidential election in order to be recognized on the ballot. That is estimated to be about 28 thousand signatures, with the requirement that at least 500 of the signatures have to come from eight of the sixteen congressional districts in the state. The signature requirements will be increased in 2015 to 1 percent. After gaining access to the ballot, a minor party will have to receive at least 2 percent of the total vote cast for the applicable office at the most recent regular election to remain on the ballot. After four years, that number will be increased to 3 percent.[4]

The Libertarian Party of Ohio filed a federal lawsuit the same week the new minor party bill was signed by Governor John Kasich. The suit focused on the retroactive nature of the bill, claiming the rules were being changed midstream. The Tea Party in Ohio was unhappy with Governor Kasich and his support of expanding Medicaid, and some of the Tea Party leaders had already decided to give their support to the Libertarian candidate for governor, former State Representative Charlie Earl. They believed that this law was passed to make it difficult for Earl to qualify as the Libertarian candidate for governor in 2014. In early January of 2014, a federal court issued an injunction against the law, and it will not be in effect for the 2014 election. Still, under current rules promulgated by the Ohio secretary of state, minor party candidates face signature requirements that are very similar to those applied to major party candidates. Among the requirements are that nominating petitions for the candidate of a party must be circulated by those who are actually members of that party and that the circulators must disclose the name of their employer. In 2014, Secretary Jon Husted determined that Libertarian candidate,

Earl; his running mate, Sherry Clark; and Libertarian candidate for attorney general, Stephen Linnabarry, had all violated these requirements and therefore could not appear on the primary ballot. Consequently, they were also barred from appearing on the general election ballot.

earlandclarkforohio.com

Party Organizations

Both of the major parties once held biennial (every two years) state conventions. The Ohio Republicans gave up holding conventions in 1988, citing the cost of the meetings as a major reason.[5] Ohio Democrats, however, have a requirement within their bylaws to hold state party conventions. Delegates to conventions are selected by local county party organizations, and they customarily adopt a platform stating the positions of the party on major issues. Party conventions in Ohio have also served to highlight candidates. At the same time, and in contrast to the process in some other states, the major party state conventions in Ohio have no legal role in the actual nomination of state candidates. The candidates must garner the correct number of statutory-required signatures to qualify for the ballot.

State laws regulate Ohio political parties. The Ohio Revised Code (ORC) says that "The controlling committees of each major political party shall be a state committee consisting of two members, one male and one female, elected every two years from each of the 33 Senate districts."[6] State senate districts are now used, and that means that the Democratic and Republican state committees consist of 66 members. An Ohio county central committee consists of one member from each election precinct in the county, or one member from each ward and township in the county. Most Ohio county parties use the precinct as the election unit for its committee members, and a number of them have moved to four-year terms. These party committee members are elected in the party primary elections that are held on even-numbered years.

The state law on party organization and function is very thin because political parties are private, nongovernmental organizations. Therefore, state laws cannot specify what officers the committees are to elect nor the duties of these officers.

Instead, these matters are spelled out in the bylaws adopted by these various party committees. The strictest regulations of parties in Ohio are in the area of campaign finance law (discussed below).

Party bylaws often permit the state or county executive committee to appoint notable members of the party who were not otherwise elected to the state or county central committee. Some of these state or county party committees might also choose to endorse candidates in primary elections. Those endorsements carry none of the benefits sometimes found in other states, such as automatic ballot access or top position on the primary ballot. The value of the party endorsement is dependent on the support the endorsing party organization invests in it. In Ohio, statewide candidates seek out the endorsement of those county organizations that choose to endorse. For Ohio Republican statewide candidates, the endorsement of the Franklin County Organization in Columbus has been viewed as quite valuable.

The only significant statutory authority granted to county committees in Ohio is the power to replace partisan-elected office holders who have vacated (or been removed) from their offices within the county. This power does not extend to judges. State statutes require that the governor of the state fill vacant judgeships. When state legislators leave office early, the respective party caucuses in the house or the senate replace them. The governor fills vacancies in other statewide administrative offices.

There are also important non-statutory party organizations in the state. The most important are the legislative party committees. The particular party caucus selects the members of these committees. These committees hire staff and, often, a political consulting firm. Their function is to recruit and elect candidates for the next election cycle. This is an arduous task that is compounded by term limits. Term limits create numerous open seats, and the legislative campaign committee is expected to recruit viable candidates in those districts deemed competitive. Recruiting legislative candidates is challenging. The best prospects are those who hold some sort of local office in the district and are able to raise some of their own funds or self-finance their own campaigns. Another pool of possible legislature candidates are former legislators who have been or are going to be termed out of office. The caucus campaign committees are also required to raise funds to support those candidates newly recruited as well as support incumbents at risk. This practice is usually termed *targeting*. Targeting is a practice of legislative campaign committees, political parties, and political action committees (PACs), which focus scarce financial resources on either candidates who have a good chance of winning or on incumbents who appear vulnerable. In an Ohio state house election, the number of contested seats, where both parties are financially engaged, is usually less than a dozen. In the 2012 election cycle, the Ohio senate legislative party committees contested only one seat where the incumbent was an appointee and the district was seen as competitive. The appointed Democratic incumbent survived that election.

Party Politics

John Fenton, in his 1966 book, *Midwest Politics*, places his study of Ohio politics in a section titled "The Job-Oriented States." According to Fenton, "the distinguishing characteristic of jobs-oriented politics is that most of the people who participate in politics on a day-to-day basis do so out of a desire for jobs or contracts rather than because of a concern for public policy."[7] That description would not capture today's Ohio political parties. A variety of factors have eroded the patronage available to Ohio parties, including civil service law, the onset of public unions, outsourcing of state work to private contractors, and—perhaps most importantly—the chilling effect of the 1990 U.S. Supreme Court decision *Rutan et al. v. Republican Party of Illinois*. In *Rutan,* the court essentially made patronage illegal, ruling that state governments violate an individual's First Amendment rights when they hire (or refuse to hire), fire, or promote state employees on the basis of political affiliation or party activity.[8] Even if patronage jobs were still available, there would not be many of them. All recent Ohio governors have been able to brag that they have reduced the number of state workers. Current Governor Kasich has pushed for privatization of state agencies, further eroding possible patronage positions. Because of this, contemporary party organizations in Ohio are not built on the patronage system that Fenton observed in the 1960s.

Still, contract seekers and interest groups continue to make demands on the state of Ohio. They no longer, however, limit their attention and donations to the political parties. Instead, they hire from the ranks of the large pool of dedicated lobbyists in Columbus. Nowadays, it is the lobbyists, rather than the political parties, who act as liaisons with elected officials. In fact, a few entrepreneurial political party chairmen are also registered lobbyists. Their fees, however, do not go the party organizations.

The Ohio Republican Party

In the mid-20th century, the Ohio Republican Party was known for being exceptionally well organized. As Fenton noted, this was partially because they realized "that they constituted a minority of the voting population of the state and were willing to submit to strong central direction of their party in order to achieve electoral victory over a disorganized majority."[9] It was also due to the talents of longtime Ohio Republican state chairman, Ray Bliss (Photo 8.2). Bliss ran the party in Ohio with an iron fist. For example, Republican Party chairs had to seek his approval before making statements to the press. Bliss was acutely aware that Republican policy positions did not always correspond with those of a majority of the Ohio electorate; his solution, for which he was famous, advocated keeping issues out of elections. He was so successful that Fenton's chapter on Ohio politics was titled "Issueless Politics in Ohio."

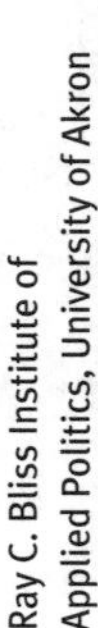

Ray Bliss

This reluctance to bring up controversial issues no longer describes today's Ohio Republican Party. In 2011, the Republican-dominated 129th general assembly took up a controversial measure to limit the collective bargaining rights of public employees in Ohio. Before the law could go into effect, it was decisively defeated in a referendum. Still, Republicans continued to push controversial legislation, including in the 130th general assembly, when the Republican legislature added a number of abortion restrictions and attempted to defund Planned Parenthood in the budget bill.

As the Republican Party has become more issues oriented, it has also become less cohesive. In the 129th general assembly, the conservative wing of the Republican Party in the legislature opposed Governor Kasich's expansion of Medicaid, which was part of the federal Affordable Care Act (Obamacare). At the time, house Speaker William Batchelder (R-Medina) said that twenty members in his Ohio house Republican caucus would rather be shot than vote for the Medicaid expansion.

Controversial and divisive issues have become much more common in the Ohio Republican Party in the 21st century. Mirroring the trend nationally, the Ohio Republican Party has become much more ideologically conservative. This conservative shift is most noticeable in the Republican caucus in the Ohio house of representatives. Representative Jay Hottinger, who entered the house in 1995, was once viewed as one of the most conservative members of that body. In a 2013 interview with the *Columbus Dispatch*, he indicated that though he had not changed, "the caucus has clearly moved significantly to the right."[10]

Statehouse observers point to gerrymandered house districts, term limits, and a more organized Tea Party movement as a reason for this shift.[11] In 1991, 2001, and 2011, when state house districts were being drawn, Republicans controlled the Ohio Apportionment Board. Although gerrymandering (discussed in Chapter 3) often works to increase the number of seats a political party is able to obtain in a legislature, it is also used to create what are known as safe political seats. Constructing politically lopsided districts (i.e., districts that contain a clear majority of Republican voters) creates safe seats. Within such districts, there is no electoral payoff to moderating one's ideology. In fact, the only major challenge to remaining in office occurs during primary elections. Groups aligned with the conservative Tea Party movement tend to be very active in Republican Party primary elections. Given that low voter turnout is the norm during primaries, Tea

Party supporters are allowed to exercise a disproportionate influence during these contests, again pushing Republican candidates toward the right.

Curiously enough, all of this has not led to a more homogeneous party. The strain between Governor Kasich and the state Republican Party organization is discussed in Chapter 4. Nowhere was this split more evident than in Kasich's decision to embrace Medicaid expansion under the Affordable Care Act, a position which was political heresy to many conservative Republicans in the state.

Vernal G. Riffe

Vernal G. Riffe

The Ohio Democratic Party

Fenton's description of the Ohio Democratic Party in the 1960s was not very glowing. He concluded, "There was, in fact, no statewide Democratic party in Ohio."[12] Rather, according to Fenton, the Democratic Party was an aggregation of city political machines, with no interest in winning statewide elections unless the candidate was from their city.

Fortunately for Democrats, this description no longer captures the modern party in Ohio. Although the party has not enjoyed much electoral success of late (with the notable exception of the 2006 elections), it has become more organized and has benefited from the support of labor unions in the state. What Fenton did not anticipate was the rise of Speaker Vernal (Vern) G. Riffe (Photo 8.3). Riffe created an effective legislative campaign organization for the Democrats. Serving as Speaker of the Ohio house of representatives from 1975 until 1995, he effectively used his position to raise funds to support the Democratic Ohio house candidates. Also important was the emergence of Richard Celeste, a Democrat who was elected governor, a position the Republican Jim Rhodes had held for most of the 1970s and 1980s. Celeste was not favored in the 1982 Democratic primary, where he faced Attorney General William Brown as well as Cincinnati councilman (and now talk TV shock host) Jerry Springer.

Celeste did have an established political base in Cleveland, where his father had run for mayor. Most importantly, he had the support of Riffe. Beyond Riffe, however, the Toledo Democratic Party organization was the only major group to support Celeste in the primary. Their leader, James Ruvolo, went on to become the Democratic state party chairperson after Celeste won the Democratic primary and easily defeated Republican Clarence "Bud" Brown in the Reagan midterm election of 1982. That 1982 Democratic primary was the last spirited statewide Democratic primary in Ohio. The Democrats began to lose their grip on Ohio government with the election of Governor George Voinovich in 1990 and the capturing of the apportionment board by the Ohio Republicans. Speaker Riffe saw the writing on the wall and took his exit.

The Republicans controlled the office of governor and most of state government for the next sixteen years. This long Republican reign broke what some called a law of Ohio politics: the law of the "regularity of gubernatorial rotation."[13] The Democrats finally made a comeback in 2006, when Congressman Ted Strickland ran virtually unopposed for the Democratic nomination and then easily defeated Republican Secretary of State Ken Blackwell. That year proved to be a banner year for Democrats in Ohio. Democrats swept all of the statewide offices except state auditor, which was won by Republican candidate Mary Taylor. Strickland pushed the Democrats to select Ohio house member Chris Redfern as the party's chairman. Redfern continues to hold that office, although he has returned to the Ohio house.

Redfern has been a constant critic of Republican Governor Kasich. He has also worked to forge a much closer alliance with organized labor, something made easier by the failed threat to public employee unionization, symbolized by the Republican-passed Senate Bill 5 (discussed in Chapter 9).

State Parties and Elections

Despite the diminished role of state parties, Ohio's state party organizations continue to act as slate makers (determining who will appear on the statewide ballot). The state Republican Party in Ohio played a critical role in constructing the successful 1990 state ticket by encouraging Bob Taft to give up his gubernatorial bid and run for secretary of state. In 2010, the state Republican Party also was able to persuade David Yost to give up a challenge to Mike DeWine for the Republican attorney general nomination and instead seek the office of state auditor. On election night, both would claim victory.

In addition to the statewide political offices, the state party organizations also recruit candidates for the Ohio supreme court elections. Of course, both parties provide services to their candidates. Ohio political parties can be a source of campaign contributions for candidates, as shown below in Table 8.1. At times, parties take on other roles. For example, in the fall of 2013, the emerging gubernatorial campaign of Ed Fitzgerald removed its hired spokesperson for the campaign, and staff in the Ohio Democratic Party took on that task.

Despite all of this, the time for strong party organizations in states such as Ohio has passed. On occasion, they do serve as forums for individual power struggles or fights to define the ideology of the party. Overall, however, statewide campaigns in Ohio have become candidate centered. It is the candidate and his or her circle of advisors rather than the parties who dominate statewide general elections in Ohio. The role of the party organization is that of a supporting actor, with the assigned task of getting out the vote. The local party activists, who are often around for decades, are placed side by side with volunteers who have come out in support of a particular candidate.

In the classic study of state political subcultures, Daniel Elazar characterized Ohio as "individualistic," meaning that political participation in Ohio was motivated by those seeking benefits.[14] As already explained, however, patronage in the form of public jobs is very rare today. Many of today's party activists are motivated instead by ideology. James Wilson has characterized this type of motivation as "purposive."[15] This change has redefined the character of Ohio politics and political parties in the 21st century.[16]

Campaign Finance in Ohio

Ohio candidates for local and state office, political parties, and other political organizations that raise money for elections are subject to state campaign finance laws that are distinct from federal campaign law. In general, one of the goals of campaign finance law is to increase transparency and allow the public to know both who is contributing money and to whom they are contributing. To achieve transparency, office seekers and other groups that spend money on elections are required to report the sources of their contributions, and political donors must report their spending. There is a pre- and postelection filing for the primary and the general election. Local candidates for office are required to file their campaign finance reports with their county boards of election while state office seekers submit their documents to the Ohio secretary of state. The press often reports how much each candidate for a particular office has raised, and this is often taken, along with polling data, as a measure of support for candidacies.

The limit on campaign contributions in Ohio is considerably higher than the federal cap. The cap is adjusted annually by the Consumer Price Index and posted on the secretary of state's website. In 2013, the cap for individuals and PACs for contributions to statewide candidates was $12,155.52. The secretary of state's contribution limits are presented in Table 8.1. There is no limit on what an individual can spend on his or her own election. There has never been a self-financed trophy-office-seeking statewide candidate in Ohio. Indeed, according to a report by the Brennan Center for Justice, "Ohio has the highest limit in the country for contributions to state legislative candidates . . . and the third highest for individual contributions to statewide candidates."[17]

As Table 8.1 shows, political parties are able to spend large sums of money for campaigns. Table 8.2 provides an example of how much money was raised by party committees in 2012.

TABLE 8.1 Ohio Campaign Contribution Limits

TO ↓ FROM → per Election Period unless otherwise footnoted	*INDIVIDUAL (must be 7 years of age or older)*	*PACS PCES*	*COUNTY PARTY state candidate fund*	*COUNTY PARTY other account8*	*STATE PARTY state candidate fund*	*LEGISLATIVE CAMPAIGN FUND*	*CAMPAIGN COMMITTEE (includes local)*
STATEWIDE	$12,155.52	$12,155.52	$303,887.961[2]	$3,038.88[9]	$685,571.24[7]	**PROHIBITED**	$12,155.52
SENATE	$12,155.52	$12,155.52	$12,155.52[1] $136,749.58[2]	$3,038.88[9]	$136,749.58[7]	$68,070.90[6] $136,749.58[6]	$12,155.52
HOUSE	$12,155.52	$12,155.52	$12,155.52[1] $68,070.90[2]	$3,038.88[9]	$68,070.90[7]	$35,258.98[6] $68,070.90[6]	$12,155.52
STATE PARTY State Candidate Fund	$36,466.56[3]	$36,466.56[3]	**No Limit**	**PROHIBITED**	**No Limit**	**No Limit**	$36,466.56[5]
LEGISLATIVE CAMPAIGN FUND	$18,233.28[3]	$18,233.28[3]	**No Limit**	**PROHIBITED**	**No Limit**	**PROHIBITED**	$18,233.28[5]
COUNTY PARTY State Candidate Fund	$12,155.52[10]	**PROHIBITED**	**PROHIBITED**	**PROHIBITED**	**No Limit**	**No Limit**	$12,155.52[4]
PACs PCEs	$12,155.52[3]	$12,155.52[13]	$12,155.52[11]	$12,155.52[11]	$12,155.52[11]	**PROHIBITED**	$12,155.52[3]

1. These limits apply to contributions given to a campaign committee which is **not** a *"designated state campaign committee"*.

2. These limits apply to cash or cash equivalents, not in-kind. The campaign committee of a house or a senate candidate which is a *'designated state campaign committee'* may accept, in aggregate, from any one or a combination of state candidate funds of county political parties **$60,777.59** and **$121,597.85**, respectively, in an election period.

3. These limits are per calendar year.

4. This limit is per calendar year and may only be made if the campaign committee's candidate will appear on a ballot in that county or is an officeholder representing any part of that county.

5. These limits are per calendar year and do not apply to contributions given by a *'designated state campaign committee'*.

6. These limits apply to cash or cash equivalents, not in-kind. The smaller limit is for the Primary election period and the larger limit is for the General election period.

7. These limits apply to cash or cash equivalents, not in-kind.

8. These limits apply to political parties in counties having a population of less than 150,000 which do not establish a State Candidate Fund. *"Other Account"* does not include an account that contains moneys received from the Ohio Political Party Fund (Restricted Fund).

9. Recipients of county party non-State Candidate Fund contributions must be campaign committees for statewide candidates or a *'designated state campaign committee'*.

10. This limit is per calendar year. Contributions to a County Party SCF are restricted to individuals residing in the county or *'designated state campaign committees'* of the County Party SCF.

11. These limits are per calendar year and apply to the aggregate of contributions given by the National, State and County level of a political party.

12. A campaign committee for a statewide candidate may **accept** not more than this amount, in aggregate, from any one or a combination of state candidate funds of county political parties in an election period.

13. This limit is per calendar year and does not apply to contributions made to or received by one or more PACs that are affiliated.

TABLE 8.2 Money Raised by Party Committees in Ohio in 2012

Ohio Democratic Party	
Committee	*Total*
Ohio Democratic Party	$12,401,827
House Democratic Caucus Fund of Ohio	$2,992,772
Ohio Senate Democrats	$292,796
Ohio Republican Party	
Committee	*Total*
Ohio Republican Party	$7,170,974
Ohio House Republican Campaign Committee	$5,771,444
Republican Senate Campaign Committee	$3,060,220

Data source: "Follow the Money," accessed October 21, 2014, http://beta.followthemoney.org/

The financial prowess of the Republican legislative campaign committees is a result of their majority status. Whichever party has majority status enjoys much greater financial support from state interest groups. Leadership and aspiring leaders are expected to donate monies from their campaign funds and raise money for their caucus.

Public Party Funds

In the 1980s, the Ohio general assembly created a system of public financing for political parties in Ohio. It is usually referred to as the *Ohio political party fund* and is supported by monies received as a result of individuals exercising the check-off option on their state income tax returns. According to Ohio law, after the costs of the audit are deducted, the tax commissioner shall "pay any moneys remaining in the fund only to political parties qualifying for them under division (B) of section 3717.17 of the Ohio Revised Code."[18] These funds must be divided equally between the qualifying parties, with half going to the treasurer of the state executive committees and the other half distributed to the treasurer of each county executive committee in "accordance with the ratio that the number of check-offs in each county bear to the total number of check-offs."[19] Only major parties as defined by the ORC may apply for public monies from the Ohio political party funds.

The amount of money in this fund has been dwindling. In 2002, 512,000 checked this box. By 2011, the number was only 261,000. Furthermore, the recipient party organizations may only use the money for administrative costs and get out the vote (GOTV) efforts. The funds cannot be used to support candidates nor to fund their campaigns.[20]

Interest Groups

An *interest group* is an organized group with common interests that attempts to achieve its goals by influencing government officials. Interest groups lobby government officials and donate funds and volunteer in political campaigns. They may also become active in a particular political party. For example, organized labor has long been involved in the Ohio Democratic Party. More recently, groups affiliated with the Tea Party movement have become a force in the Ohio Republican Party. The activities that Ohio interest groups and their lobbyists use to influence policy outcomes are the same in most states and at the national level. They include the following:

1. **Becoming involved in political campaigns**

These efforts are usually primarily financial. Interest groups can form PACs to make donations directly to campaigns or campaign committees. Interest groups with access to other, nonfinancial assets can also deploy those resources in campaigns. Labor unions, for example, can organize their members for and against candidates by using endorsements and by mobilizing members. The National Rifle Association, one of the most dominant groups in Ohio, is able to push its members to vote for favored candidates. This is also true for groups opposing or favoring abortion rights.

2. **Testifying in front of legislative committees**

The value of this testimony is questionable; however, it is one way that lobbyists show their employer that they are doing something to earn their pay.

3. **Making informal contacts**

Lobbyists representing interest groups will often reach out to lawmakers, providing them with information and opinions on pending legislation.

4. **Sponsoring initiatives and referendum petitions**

Gambling interests managed to successfully place an initiative on the ballot in 2009, allowing casinos to be operated in the state. In 2011, public unions were able to use the referendum to block a law restricting their collective bargaining rights.

5. **Participating in direct advocacy**

Interest groups often encourage members to write letters, send e-mails, or make phone calls to legislators, urging them to favor or oppose legislation.

6. **Seeking publicity**

There are various ways to gain publicity for an issue or set of issues. Sometimes, for example, interest groups will organize protest marches and other demonstrations to gain publicity.

Fredric Bolotin observed that Ohio is "a state where groups have significant influence but no single group or set of groups dominate the policy process."[21] So many different interest groups vie for power in Ohio that no one dominant interest group is able to emerge. As has been the case nationwide, Ohio has seen a proliferation of interest groups and interest group activity. In particular, there has been a great deal of interest group activity surrounding the expansion of Medicaid (a joint federal and state program) in Ohio. Hospital associations and groups advocating for low-income groups have pushed for this legislation, while the Tea Party actively opposes expansion. There are also new groups that have become very active and influential in Ohio, including gambling interests and the oil and gas interests that are interested in a process known as fracking (see Box 4.1).

There has also been a significant rise of single-issue groups in Ohio. A single-issue group is a type of interest group organized around a particular cause. Examples of single-interest groups in Ohio include environmentally conscious activists who have held rallies and protests in Columbus against fracking. Pro-life and pro-choice groups have also been very active over the years in Columbus. At the same time, lobbying activity by corporations, universities, and state and local governments has also increased in recent decades.

Lobbyists who register as legislative agents represent interest groups in Ohio. One type of legislative agent is called a *legislative liaison*. Legislative liaisons represent state agencies, boards, and commissions. There is also a registered legislative liaison for the governor's office. Although legislative liaisons must register as legislative agents, they are frequently not thought of as lobbyists by the legislators. A second type of legislative agent is an *in-house lobbyist*, who represents one interest. The Ohio Council of Retail Merchants, for example, employs an in-house lobbyist who works to promote the interests of retail merchants with the Ohio government. There are also citizen lobbyists. These lobbyists are fighting for a cause and therefore do not seek remuneration. A group of lobbyists whose appearance is relatively recent yet who wield noticeable influence are known as *contract lobbyists*. These registered agents represent a number of clients.

Tom Suddes, a columnist for the *Plain Dealer* and a journalism professor at Ohio University, took a look at the fortunes of some contract lobbyists who had ties to Governor Kasich. The first one mentioned by Suddes is Donald Thibaut, who served as Kasich's aide in the Ohio senate and then as chief of staff when he went to Congress in 1983. In May 2009, Thibaut had zero clients. In May 2011, after Kasich won, Thibaut had twelve clients, including American Electric Power (a significant electric power distributor in Ohio), Medical Mutual of Ohio, Corrections Corporation of America, and GTECH, the lottery and gaming vendor whose products include video lottery (electric slot) machines. Suddes also described the gain in clients for Robert Klaffky, who heads Van Meter, Ashbrook & Associates. The firm was founded by Tom Van Meter, a leader of the conservative wing of the Republican Party in the 1980s. Klaffky, according to Suddes, had ties to Speaker Batchelder. After Kasich became governor, Klaffky went from eight clients to twenty-three clients. Those who hired his services include First Energy, the Wholesale Beer and Wine Association of Ohio, and the Columbus-based IQ Innovations, which is involved in online education. Suddes also looked at who was not "in." One of those most definitely "out" during the early years of the Kasich administration was Kimberly Redfern, the wife of the chair of the Ohio Democratic Party. In May of 2009, she had sixteen clients, one of which was MTR Gaming Group, owners of Scioto Downs, one of the horse racetracks seeking permission to have slot machines. By 2011, she had lost all of her clients.[22]

Not all of those who are members of Ohio's statehouse lobbying community thrive because of their political ties. John Mahaney, who retired in 2013 after fifty-five years of representing the 4,500 Ohio Retail Merchants Association, said at the time of his retirement that he was a force on Capital Square for the following reasons: "We tell the truth, we keep our commitments and we're loyal."[23]

One of the figures who seems to appear in all academic and press reports on Ohio government and politics is contract lobbyist Neil Clark. Clark served as an aide to former Ohio Senate President Stanley Aronoff, and capitalized on the contacts and knowledge he had gained as an aide to become arguably the most influential contract lobbyist in recent decades in Ohio. His current list of clients is presented in Box 8.1. The list of clients provides a sample of some of the types of interest groups that are active in Columbus that hire contract lobbyists. He is able to maintain influence because of his ties to the Republican majority in the Ohio senate.

BOX 8.1: Selected List of Clients of Neil Clark

21 Entertainment

Absolute Pharmacy

ACE Cash Express

(Continued)

(Continued)

Austen BioInnovation Institute in Akron
CheckSmart Financial
Cincinnati Public Schools
EverPower Wind Holdings
Fair Gaming Coalition of Ohio
Frontier Ohio
Halcyon Solutions Inc.
Liberty Healthcare Corporation
Museum of Contemporary Art Cleveland
Ohio Association of Community Colleges
Ohio Association of Convention & Visitors Bureaus
Ohio Cable Telecommunications Association
Ohio Health Care Association
Ohio Society of Certified Public Accountants
Ohio Soft Drink Association
Ohio State ACE
Public Finance Authority
Republic Steel
Rhino Bill
Salon Schools Group
Time Warner Cable Midwest LLC
Wholesale Beer & Wine Association of Ohio

Source: Joint Legislative Ethics Committee Agents List, accessed May 15, 2013, http://www2.jlec-olig.state.oh.us/olac/Reports/FormsFiled.aspx?id=90&type=a

Regulation of Interest Groups

At one time, lobbying the executive branch in Ohio was unregulated. Because of concerns about the granting of unbid contracts by the Controlling Board, executive branch and controlling board lobbying began to be regulated in 1991, and reporting is now required. There were additional significant changes made to the law in 1994 as a result of more bad publicity. It was reported that certain members of the legislature were demanding $500 honoraria for attending meetings with interest groups. Often, through a process known as *pancaking*, multiple $500 honorariums were collected for the same event. The 1994 law ended all honorariums, even those falling below the old $500 threshold. Moreover, the law stipulated that all lobbyist-paid travel and lodging expenses in and out of Ohio are to be reported. Restrictions on the "wining and dining" of legislators by lobbyists were also imposed. Money spent on gifts and dinners for legislators has to be reported to the Office of the Legislative Inspector General and the bipartisan twelve-member Legislative Joint Ethics Committee. The committee itself was a creation of the law. All gifts that exceed $25 in value must be reported to the committee, and officials are not allowed to accept any gifts over $75. Finally, a "revolving door" limit was imposed on office holders, who must now wait one year out of office before they can engage in lobbying.

Elections

Elections in Ohio are conducted by the eighty-eight county Election Boards, which are organized by state statute. The Ohio County Election boards are governed by four-member boards, which must have two Democrats and two Republicans. The two members from each major party are nominated by the local party's executive committee and then appointed by the secretary of state to a four-year term. Their pay is modest and determined by county population. It is customary for the chair of the local party committees to sit on these county Election Boards as some compensation for their work for the party. The Election Boards were designed in this way to create a system of checks and balances, with Democrats and Republicans keeping an eye on each other's partisan actions. There are also to be an equal number of full-time and part-time Democrats and Republicans employed at the board, and this is the last vestige of political patronage in Ohio, since the employees are selected by the boards and each party defers to the other party's choice. The board draws the precinct boundaries used to poll the voters. The board also selects the type of election technology used in casting ballots and tabulating results. The voting systems have to be preapproved by the secretary of state. In the case of a tie on the Elections Board in Ohio, which usually results as a dispute between the two local parties, the secretary of state casts the tie-breaking vote.

In order to vote in Ohio, a person must register thirty days prior to the election and must be at least eighteen years old at the time of the next general election. As an example, a seventeen-year-old can register and vote in a primary to nominate candidates only if they are going to be eighteen before the next general election. It was once the case that voter registration in Ohio was required only in larger municipalities. After 1977, however, due to a statewide initiative, everyone who wants to vote in Ohio must first register.

In recent years, there has been an ongoing battle in Ohio over when, prior to Election Day, voters will be allowed to cast their ballots. Ohio has gradually moved to allow early voting. Early voting can take one of two forms. First, voters may cast what are called *absentee ballots* by mail. Allowing absentee ballots is not new, but what has changed is that voters no longer have to provide an excuse to make use of absentee voting. Alternatively, voters have been allowed to vote prior to Election Day at their county board of elections. This has been a source of controversy (see Box 8.2), particularly in presidential elections, where Ohio is seen as a decisive battleground state.

BOX 8.2: Early Voting in Ohio

On Election Day in November of 2004, many Ohio voters faced long lines at their polling stations. The following year, in order to try to head off future problems and expedite voting, the Ohio general assembly changed the state's voting laws and adopted what is called *early in-person (EIP) voting*. EIP is really a form of absentee voting where voters do not have to show up at their local precinct on Election Day in order to cast their ballots. While Ohio had long made absentee voting available for those who were unable to get to the polls on the actual day of the election, before this change in the law, a voter was required to first provide a valid reason why he or she was unavailable on Election Day. Also, absentee ballots, for those who had qualified, were generally mailed to the local board of elections.

The 2005 law changed all of this. First, Ohio adopted "no-fault" absentee voting. Every voter was eligible to cast an absentee ballot without having to offer a reason. Second, voters, although still able to mail in their votes, could also visit their local board of elections or other designated location before Election Day to cast their absentee vote in person. Technically, this is what the term EIP voting means.

Under the new law, county election boards were required to begin accepting early votes thirty-five days before the election. Since Ohioans may register to vote up to thirty days before an election, the result was a five-day period in which individuals could both register to vote and actually cast their vote on the same day. This five-day period became known as *Golden Week*. Golden Week immediately generated controversy, with opponents arguing that voting officials would not have time to verify a registration before allowing someone to vote.[1]

Although EIP did not appreciably increase voter turnout in Ohio, nearly 30 percent of the Ohio electorate did choose to cast their ballots in this manner in 2008.[2] It was clear, however, that EIP voting was not evenly distributed across demographic groups and party members. A study by the Bliss Institute of Politics at the University of Akron noted that, "[i]n terms of demographic characteristics, early voters were more likely than election-day voters to be women, older, and of lower income and education attainment." Perhaps most importantly, the study found that "early voters appear to have favored Democratic candidates in 2010 and 2006, while election-day voters favored Republican candidates."[3]

In 2011, Republicans in the general assembly passed House Bill 194, which would have reduced the days when EIP voting would be available before Election Day from thirty-five to seventeen (thereby eliminating Golden Week). The actual number of days available would only be 14, since House Bill 194 also prohibited EIP voting on the weekend and Monday before an election.[4] The bill never went into effect because opponents gathered enough signatures to challenge the law by referendum (referendums are explained in Chapter 9). Rather than have the law challenged on the ballot, the general assembly replaced House Bill 194 before the 2012 election with Senate Bill 295. Since the old law was repealed, it would no longer be subject to a referendum (although this was the subject of much legal debate). Senate Bill 295 brought back Golden Week and all of the EIP voting days except for the last weekend and Monday before the election.[5] The latter limitation was successfully challenged by the Obama campaign, with Federal District Court Judge Peter Economus issuing an injunction in August of 2012 that restored EIP voting on these last three days before the 2012 election.[6]

In February of 2014, the Ohio legislature again passed a bill eliminating Golden Week. Later in that same month, Ohio Secretary of State Jon Husted issued a directive listing the allowable EIP voting hours for all of the eighty-eight county boards of election in Ohio. This directive included no Sunday hours or evening hours nor did it allow for EIP voting on the Monday before the election. The Obama campaign again went to Judge Economus, who ordered Husted to allow for EIP voting hours on the three days leading up to the election. Husted then issued a new directive, which attempted to comply with this order by adding hours on the Saturday and Monday before the election. African American church leaders in Ohio were still unhappy. In particular, they were upset about the lack of Sunday voting hours. Since 2008, African American churches had maintained an active "Souls to the Polls" campaign, where the churches would transport their members to polls to vote early.[7] The NAACP in Ohio challenged both the law eliminating Golden Week and Husted's new directive as violating the Equal Protection Clause of the Constitution and Section 2 of the Voting Rights Act. Judge Economus again issued an injunction ordering the Secretary of State to set additional evening and Sunday hours and restoring Golden Week. The 6th Circuit Court of Appeals, however, upheld the ruling.[8] The United States Supreme Court stayed Judge Economus' decision, and the 2014 general election in Ohio took place without a Golden Week, with only four hours of EIP voting on one Sunday and with no EIP voting hours on the Monday before Election Day.[9]

(Continued)

(Continued)

Notes

1. Robert Higgs, "Ohio Senate Votes to Reduce Days for Early Voting, Eliminate So-Called 'Golden Week,'" *Cleveland.com*, November 20, 2013, accessed November 11, 2014, http://www.cleveland.com/open/index.ssf/2013/11/ohio_senate_votes_to_reduce_da.html
2. Joe Vardon, "Early Voting Hasn't Boosted Ohio Turnout," *Columbus Dispatch*, June 16, 2014, accessed November 11, 2014, http://www.dispatch.com/content/stories/local/2014/06/16/early-voting-hasntboosted-ohio-turnout.html. See also *Obama for America v. Husted*, 697 F.3d 423 (6th Cir. 2012) at 426.
3. "A Study of Early Voting in Ohio Elections," Ray C. Bliss Institute of Applied Politics, University of Akron, accessed November 11, 2014, http://www.uakron.edu/bliss/research/archives/2010/EarlyVotingReport.pdf
4. Lynda J. Jacobsen, "Ohio Legislative Service Commission Final Analysis," accessed November 11, 2014, http://www.lsc.state.oh.us/analyses129/11-hb194-129.pdf
5. John Guillan, "Ohio House Votes to Repeal Controversial Election Law," *Cleveland.com*, May 8, 2012, accessed November 11, 2014, http://www.cleveland.com/open/index.ssf/2012/05/ohio_house_votes_to_repeal_con.html
6. *Obama for America v. Husted*, Case No. 2:12-CV-0636 (August 31, 2012).
7. Andrew Tobias, "Black Clergy Protest Elimination of 'Souls to the Polls' and Evening Early Voting in 2014 (VIDEO)," *Cleveland.com*, March 6, 2014, accessed November 11, 2014, http://www.cleveland.com/cuyahoga-county/index.ssf/2014/03/black_clergy_protest_elmination_of_sunday_souls_to_the_polls_early_voting_in_2014_video.html
8. "Appeals Panel Upholds Ohio Ruling Allowing Early Voting," September 24, 2014, accessed November 11, 2014, http://triblive.com/politics/politicalheadlines/6856380-74/early-voting-state#axzz3IiBFhqD2
9. Jackie Borchardt, "Supreme Court Blocks Early Voting in Ohio," *Cleveland.com*, September 29, 2014, accessed November 11, 2014, http://www.cleveland.com/open/index.ssf/2014/09/supreme_court_blocks_early_vot.html

The Primary

A *primary* is an election held before the general election to nominate a political party's candidates for office. Primaries replaced caucuses (meetings of party supporters) as means to nominate candidates rather early in Ohio. Direct primaries were mandated for most elective offices in Ohio in 1912. Currently, Ohio uses what is known as a *semi-closed* primary. States with open primaries allow voters to cast a vote in any party's primary without a public declaration. States with closed primaries require party declaration prior to the primary election. In Ohio, there is a public declaration and public record of which party ballot voters select. A voter, however, is allowed to change party affiliation or declare for a particular party on the day of the primary.

Ohio uses a plurality electoral system; the candidate who receives the most votes, whether or not that amounts to a majority of the votes cast, will be that party's nominee. Normally, the Ohio primary is scheduled for the first Tuesday after the first Monday in May. That changes in presidential election years, however, where Ohio has adopted the first Tuesday after the first Monday in March as primary day. States prefer to schedule early presidential primary votes in hopes that voting will not take place after a candidate has already secured enough delegates to render his or her nomination a foregone conclusion. Despite that earlier date, however, Ohio has not played a very significant role in nominating presidential candidates.

Those who want to file as independents, without any party affiliation, are permitted to run for office in Ohio. They must, however, file their signatures before the date of the primary election. This is often described as the "sore loser law," since it prevents candidates defeated in a primary from attempting to get on the general election ballot by filing to run as independents.

General Election

Even in nonfederal years (odd-numbered years), Ohio follows the federal pattern in determining when to hold a general election. Elections are held on the first Tuesday after the first Monday in November. In keeping with a 1949 state constitutional amendment, Ohio employs what is called an *office-bloc ballot*. This means that the names of candidates are listed under the office that they are seeking. Party designation is listed under the name of the candidate. The 1949 amendment abolished the old *straight ticket* arrangement, where candidates' names were arranged by party. With a few notable exceptions, such as township trustees and school boards, Ohio uses single-member district plurality elections; that is, only one office holder is elected from a district, and the candidate who receives the more votes than anyone else wins the seat.

Special Elections

Special elections are elections other than those specified above. A special election may be held only on the first Tuesday after the first Monday in February, May, August, or November or on the day authorized by a particular municipal or county charter for the holding of a primary. These defined special election dates were specified to avoid the overuse of the election system, particularly by school districts. Prior to this statute, school districts were repetitively placing property tax levies before voters. Special elections have to be held in Ohio (as in all states) to fill the remaining term of vacated seats to congressional seats. Ohio governors can appoint individuals to fill vacancies to U.S. senate seats from Ohio. This has not happened since the 1970s, when Governor John Gilligan appointed U.S. Senator Howard Metzenbaum over former astronaut (and later, senator) John Glenn.

Conclusion

One of the reasons that Ohio functions as a bellwether state in presidential years is that the state is somewhat of a microcosm of the nation. As this chapter shows, Ohio's politics mirror those of the nation. The major parties have become more polarized and paradoxically less homogenous. Money and interest groups play an ever-expanding role in governing and in elections. Battle lines between Republicans and Democrats have increasingly been drawn over election laws. While all of these statements can be made about Ohio, they can also be made about the United States in general.

Notes

1. Donald J. Ratcliffe, *The Politics of Long Division: The Birth of the Second Party System in Ohio, 1818–1828,* (Columbus: Ohio State University Press, 2000).
2. Libertarian Party of Ohio v. Blackwell, 462 F.3d 579 (6th Cir. 2006)
3. Husted Secretary of State 2013 Ohio Candidate Requirement Guide. The secretary of state's office was contacted on March 7, 2013, to further discuss this requirement.
4. Emily E. Wendel, *Sub. S.B. 193 Ohio Legislative Service Commission Bill Analysis,* accessed October 21, 2014, http://www.lsc.state.oh.us/analyses130/s0193-rh-130.pdf
5. Interview with former Republican State Chair Bob Bennett at the Bliss Center Conference, Akron, Ohio, November 7, 2013.
6. Ohio Revised Code 3517.03.
7. John H. Fenton, *Midwest Politics* (New York: Holt, Rinehart and Winston, 1966), 115.
8. William Binning, "Changing Patterns of Ohio Politics" in *Government, Politics, and Public Policy in Ohio*, ed. Carl Lieberman (Akron: Midwest Press), 35.
9. Fenton, *Midwest Politics,* 133.
10. Jim Siegel, "At the Statehouse, a Sharp Right Turn," *Columbus Dispatch,* September 15, 2013.
11. Ibid.
12. Fenton, *Midwest Politics*, 137.
13. David E. Sturrock, Michael Margolis, John C. Green, and Dick Kimmins, "Ohio Elections and Political Parties in the 1990s" in *Ohio Politics*, eds. Alexander P. Lamis and Brian Usher, 2nd ed. (Kent: Kent State University Press, 2007), 484.

14. Daniel J. Elazar, *American Federalism: A View from the States* (New York: Crowell, 1966).
15. James Q. Wilson, *Political Organizations* (Princeton: Princeton University Press, 1995), 34–35.
16. Kevin Smith and Adam Greenblatt, *Governing States and Localities* (Washington DC: Congressional Quarterly Press, 2014), 11
17. Brennan Center for Justice Report, *Campaign Finance in Ohio* (New York: Brennan Center for Justice at NYU School of Law, 2007), 7. http://www.breannancenter.org
18. Ohio Revised Code 3517.16
19. Ohio Revised Code 2517.17
20. Ohio Revised Code 3517.18
21. Fredric N. Bolotin, "Interest Groups in Ohio" in *Government, Politics, and Public Policy in Ohio*, ed. Carl Lieberman (Akron: Midwest Press, 1995), 107.
22. Tom Suddes, "Lobbying Right Now," *Columbus* 37, no. 7 (2011).
23. Joe Hallett, "Lobbyist Known as 'The Chief' Gets Laughs—and Respect—at Statehouse," *Columbus Dispatch*, November 13, 2013.

CHAPTER 9

Direct Democracy in Ohio

> The legislative power of the state shall be vested in a General Assembly consisting of a Senate and House of Representatives but the people reserve to themselves the power to propose to the General Assembly laws and amendments to the constitution, and to adopt or reject the same at the polls on a referendum vote as hereinafter provided. They also reserve the power to adopt or reject any law, section of any law or any item in any law appropriating money passed by the General Assembly, except as herein after provided; and independent of the General Assembly to propose amendments to the constitution and to adopt or reject the same at the polls.
>
> The Ohio Constitution, Article II, Section 1

Ohio is one of the states significantly influenced at the turn of the 20th century by the progressive movement. A good example of this was in 1912, when Ohio voters adopted a proposed amendment to the Ohio constitution providing for the initiative and the referendum. Ohio's progressivism, however, has always been somewhat muted. The state, for example, never adopted the recall (allowing voters to remove elected officials before the end of their term), which was also part of the progressive direct democracy movement of that era. The recall is, however, found in some city charters in Ohio. Dennis Kucinich, later a member of Congress and a candidate for the Democratic nomination for president, faced a recall vote as mayor of Cleveland in 1978. He survived the challenge by a margin of only 236 votes.

The Initiative

The initiative in Ohio allows citizens to initiate both constitutional amendments and state laws by signing petitions and then voting on the proposals. The procedures for amending the Ohio constitution by initiative (a direct initiative) are slightly different from those required to add a state law (an indirect initiative).

Former Cleveland Mayor Dennis Kucinich

Constitutional Amendments

There are two independent sets of signature requirements when citizens seek to amend their constitution through the initiative process. First, before signatures can be gathered in support of placing an initiated amendment on the ballot, the Ohio attorney general is required to certify that the language summarizing the proposed amendment is fair and truthful. A petition signed by at least 1,000 Ohio voters must accompany the submission to the attorney general, along with the names of three to five individuals who will represent the petitioners. After certifying the summary, the attorney general sends both it and the text of the actual amendment to the Ohio Ballot Board. This is a five-member board consisting of the secretary of state along with two Democrats and two Republicans. The board's role is to ensure that the proposed amendment does not violate the Ohio requirement that initiatives address only one subject (the single-subject rule).

Once the summary and text of the proposed amendment have been certified, new signatures must be gathered. In order for an amendment to be placed before the voters, signatures equal to 10 percent of the total number of voters who cast ballots in the most recent gubernatorial election must be gathered and submitted to the secretary of state. There is also a distributional requirement that signatures equal to 5 percent of the gubernatorial vote must be obtained in half (44) of Ohio's 88 counties (see Table 9.1). If these requirements are met, the proposed constitutional amendment is placed on the ballot in the next general election and must be approved by a majority of those voting on the issue.

This procedure for a constitutional amendment is considered a *direct initiative*, since it does not have to be submitted to the general assembly for approval before it is placed on the ballot.[1] Ohio is only one of eighteen states that allow its citizens to propose constitutional amendments through the use of the initiative.

State Laws

The 1912 constitutional amendment that gave the citizens of Ohio the right to use the initiative for constitutional amendments also permitted the citizens of

Ohio the opportunity to use the initiative to place proposed state law before the voters. The process for initiated state laws begins in the same way as constitutional amendments, with 1,000 signatures being gathered and approvals gained from the attorney general and the ballot board. In this case, the promoters must collect the signatures of 3 percent of the voters in the last gubernatorial campaign in support of their proposed statute, including 1.5 percent of the votes cast in each of at least forty-four counties. If the signatures are found to be sufficient by the secretary of state, then the proposed law goes to the general assembly. If the general assembly either amends or fails to act on the proposed law within four months, then the promoters have the option of again collecting the same number and distribution of signatures as had been required to place the matter before the general assembly. If they manage to have these second sets of signatures certified by the secretary of state, the proposed law is then placed on the ballot. If the measure receives a majority of the vote cast, it then becomes a law.

The governor cannot veto laws proposed by initiative petition and approved by the voters. Because the proposed law must first go to the general assembly, this type of initiative is termed an *indirect initiative.* In Ohio, the indirect initiative promoting state statutes has been used much less frequently than the direct initiative, which offers constitutional amendments directly to the voters and does not require that they be presented to the general assembly.

The Referendum

The final piece of Ohio's direct democracy that was adopted as a result of the constitutional convention in 1912 was the *referendum.* This word has a distinct meaning in Ohio's constitution. It gives the people the power to challenge laws that have recently been enacted by the general assembly. The referendum is very similar to an executive veto, but in this case, it is exercised by the voters. The petition challenge must be filed with the secretary of state within ninety days after the governor files the law with the secretary of state. The particular law or part of a law that is being challenged under this referendum language in the Ohio constitution is suspended from going into effect during the process of collecting the signatures and while a vote is held to accept or reject a law.

Those seeking to challenge an Ohio law using the referendum process must collect signatures equal to 6 percent of those who participated in the last gubernatorial election, while at the same time gathering signatures equal to 3 percent of the gubernatorial vote in at least forty-four counties. Once the signatures are certified, voters are asked to vote "yes" in favor of the challenged law or "no" if they are opposed. While this constitutional right of the people is used infrequently in Ohio, political commentators believe a "no" vote is easier to achieve than a "yes" vote in a referendum test.

TABLE 9.1 Signature Requirements for Initiatives and Referendums in Ohio

	For Certification by Secretary of State	*Total Percentage of Last Gubernatorial Vote*	*Minimum Percentage per County (44 of 88 Counties)*
Initiated Statutes	1,000	3*	1.5*
Initiated Amendments	1,000	10	5
Referendum	1,000	6	3

*These signatures must be gathered twice if the general assembly does not act and the measure is placed on the ballot.

Data source: "Initiative and Referendum Signature Requirements," Ohio Attorney General's Office, http://www.ohioattorneygeneral.gov/Legal/Ballot-Initiatives/Initiative-and-Referendum-Signature-Requirements

The most notable recent referendum focused on Senate Bill 5, put on the ballot as Issue 2. Senate Bill 5 challenged a law passed by the Ohio Republican-dominated general assembly in 2011, which limited collective bargaining rights of public employees. The challenge, mounted by Ohio's public employee unions, was defeated in the November 2011 general election and therefore never went into effect. Many analysts believe that the anger generated among union members by Senate Bill 5 and the resulting referendum campaign spilled over into the 2012 presidential race, which benefited Democrats in the Ohio election.

There are some laws in Ohio that are not subject to this procedure. Laws that provide for tax levies, appropriations for current state expenses, and emergency laws necessary for the preservation of public peace, health, or safety are immune from being challenged by referendum. Emergency laws require a two-thirds vote of the general assembly and go into effect immediately upon signing by the governor.

Below is a sampling of some of the more notable Ohio initiative and referendum campaigns.[2]

Right to Work

One issue that has received considerable attention in Ohio and has been addressed through the direct democracy instruments described above is the issue of *right to work*. Ohio has long had what it calls *closed shop statutes*. These statutes require all employees who are part of the bargaining unit of a union to pay the equivalent of union dues, regardless of whether they desire to be members of the union. An employee can pay what is called an *agency fee* if they have some reservation about belonging to a union, but there can be no free riders. This also means that the unions have considerable financial resources available for political campaigns. In 1985, when Richard Celeste was governor, collective bargaining rights including closed shop regulations were extended to Ohio public sector employees.

Use of the tools of direct democracy directed at right to work has a long history in Ohio. In 1958, major business leaders in Ohio decided to promote right to work and used the constitutional amendment initiative process to place the issue on the Ohio ballot. If a majority had voted for their initiative, the closed shop regulations would have ended for all Ohio workers. This initiative was promoted despite the opposition of prominent Republican Senator John Bricker and nationally renowned Ohio Republican Chair Ray Bliss. The issue was supported by the Canton-based Timken Rolling Bearing Company and General Electric, which had a presence in many places in Ohio, particularly in the Cincinnati area. The constitutional amendment by initiative was decisively rejected by a vote of 2,001,512 "no" votes to 1,106,324 "yes" votes. The Ohio Republican Party, which dominated the statewide offices at the time, was decisively defeated in that midterm election year, including Senator Bricker.

In a sense, history repeated itself after the midterm election of 2010, when the Ohio Republican Party was swept back into office. The Republicans had long controlled the Ohio senate with a sizable majority. In this election, the Republicans took back the Ohio house they had lost in 2006 and selected conservative William Batchelder as Speaker of the house. Republican John Kasich was also elected Ohio governor, ousting the incumbent Democrat Ted Strickland. This new group of Ohio Republicans forgot the lesson of 1958 and seemed unaware of the opportunity for Ohio unions to challenge new legislation with the referendum. The Republicans forged ahead and passed Senate Bill 5 (discussed above). Issue 2, which was how the referendum opposing Senate Bill 5 appeared on the ballot, lost. The split in the voting, with about 60 percent of voters going against the law and 40 percent in support, bore an uncanny resemblance to the vote cast in 1958 on the right to work initiative. Interestingly John Fenton, who studied the 1958 right to work vote, identified Holmes County as one of the few counties that voted yes in 1958.[3] That county also voted yes in 2011.

SEIU

Ohio Firefighters Protesting Senate Bill 5

The issue of right to work in Ohio continues to gain some attention because of the adoption of right to work in neighboring Michigan and Indiana as well as the restrictions passed on public employee unions in Wisconsin. The argument, made by groups such as the Ohio Chamber of Commerce, is that the lack of right to work in Ohio puts the state at a competitive disadvantage when trying to convince companies to open up businesses in the state. Nevertheless, in the lead-up to the 2014 general election, and perhaps learning from 2011 (and 1958), Governor Kasich and the Republican-dominated general assembly had little interest in pushing for right to work in Ohio. Nevertheless, Ohio union leaders have worked hard to convince their members that if Kasich and the Republicans won again in 2014, they would enact right to work in the lame duck session to boost Governor Kasich's presidential stock with national Republicans. Of course, if the union leaders' conspiracy theory is correct, then Ohioans are likely to see a third right to work referendum in 2015.

Same-Sex Marriage

There have not been many social issues addressed by the initiative and referendums in Ohio. The exception has been the issue of gay marriage. In November 2004, an initiative that proposed a constitutional amendment to define marriage was placed on the ballot. The language said,

> Only a union between one man and one woman may be a marriage valid in or recognized by this state and its political subdivisions. These state and its political subdivisions shall not create or recognize a legal status for relationships of an unmarried individual that intends to approximate the design qualities, significance or effect of marriage.[4]

"Yes" votes numbered 3,329,335 while "no" votes totaled 2,065,464. Since this was an initiative and not a referendum, this meant that the amendment prevailed.

There was suspicion in many quarters that this initiative was the handiwork Karl Rove, who was the architect of George W. Bush's presidential campaigns and who saw this initiative in Ohio as a means of increasing the turnout of social conservatives in a battleground state. Whether Rove had any hand in this issue or not, it does point to the possibility that initiatives might be placed on the ballot to achieve outcomes beyond the obvious one stated in the proposed initiative. While recent polling data suggest that Ohioans are becoming more accepting of gay marriage, the lesbian, gay, bisexual, and transgender (LGBT) community in Ohio is divided over when an initiative constitutional amendment should be placed on the ballot in Ohio to overturn the 2004 initiative.

Gambling

One of the most persistent and costly initiatives in Ohio has been over the issue of legalized gambling. On November 6, 1990, the first constitution amendment related to gambling in Ohio was proposed by initiative petition. The amendment was to

> authorize the licensing of a casino resort hotel, including games by electronic and mechanical devices, for profit, in the City of Lorain as a pilot project for a period not yet specified, but for not less than five years, if approved by the voters of the City of Lorain pursuant to laws required to be enacted by the general assembly.[5]

If the pilot program in Lorain was determined to be a success, then gambling would be expanded, with the state divided into seven districts and one casino licensed to operate in each district. This limited proposal to allow gaming in Lorain failed by a vote of 1,620,373 to 2,098,725.

In 1996, a constitutional amendment by initiative petition was placed on the ballot to allow riverboat casino gambling in Ohio. This practice was allowed by other states on the Ohio River, and it was argued that Ohio was losing out on revenue and jobs. Governor George Voinovich, an ardent opponent of legalized gambling, led a strong campaign against the amendment. Many Ohio religious leaders joined him in his campaign. Once again, Ohio voters rejected gambling, this time by just over 1 million votes.

The pro-gambling interests in the state persisted, and in November of 2006, a constitutional amendment by initiative petition was again placed on the Ohio ballot. This amendment would have allowed limited gambling, with the proceeds earmarked to provide funding for education and scholarships. This amendment failed, but only by about half a million voters. The narrowing margin may have given the gambling interests hope because two years later, they again used the initiative, this time to place on the ballot an amendment allowing a casino to be operated near Wilmington in southwest Ohio. The amendment promised to distribute to all Ohio counties the proceeds from a tax on this new casino. This effort failed with 3,466,574 voting against the amendment compared to 2,092,074 for gambling.

Finally, in November of 2009, pro-gambling forces were successful in using the initiative to place an amendment on the ballot that garnered the votes of a majority of Ohioans, passing by a vote of 1,713,200 to 1,519,636. The amendment was approved in the heart of the Great Recession with the promise of jobs for Ohioans and revenue for Ohio's cash-strapped local governments and schools.

The passage of a gambling initiative was not the work of citizens taking matters in their own hands because of a corrupt or indolent legislature; rather, this was driven by gaming interest groups, specifically Penn Ventures (a subsidiary of Penn National Gaming) and Rock Ohio Ventures LLC (run by Cleveland Cavaliers owner Dan Gilbert). Together, they spent over $50 million dollars campaigning for the amendment. They did not have the airwaves to themselves, however, since gaming interests in nearby West Virginia, threatened by this possible new venture, spent a large sum in opposition to the Ohio initiative.

This particular constitutional amendment authorized one casino facility at a specific location within each of the identified four cities: Cincinnati, Cleveland, Columbus, and Toledo. This had the effect of granting the already identified owners a monopoly. The language specified the tax rate on gross revenues and also stipulated how those funds would be distributed. Now that voters had approved the amendment, 51 percent of the tax windfall would be distributed to all eighty-eight counties based on their respective populations. Half of each county's distribution would go to its largest city (if that city had a population over 80,000). Thirty-four percent was to be distributed among all public school districts, 5 percent will go to the host cities, 3 percent to the Casino Control Commission, 3 percent to the Ohio State Racing Commission, and 2 percent to law enforcement training fund and the problem gambling and addiction fund. Each initial licensed casino also paid a single $50,000,000 fee to be used for state job-training purposes.

There are even more specifications, but the most noteworthy policy point is that the institution of state government had virtually no control over determining the location, the tax, the fees, and how the revenue to public entities would be disbursed or spent. This provides a very good example of an interest group capturing the initiative process and using it to effectively grant themselves a monopoly while at the same time limiting the regulatory authority of the Ohio state government. Unfortunately for the state, the revenues predicted from the four casinos and the promise of money to local governments and schools continue to decline rather than grow.[6]

Redistricting

As discussed in Chapter 3, Ohio has a very partisan system for drawing state and federal legislative districts. These redistricting processes have been in place for some time, and the party out of power in Ohio often uses the initiative constitutional amendment process to offer up what it calls a fair or nonpartisan scheme for redistricting. These efforts have been undertaken, with no success to boast of, by both of the major parties in Ohio.

In 1981, the Ohio Republicans supported an initiative constitutional amendment to create a commission that would have been required to emphasize the compactness of districts when drawing state and federal lines. That effort failed with

1,513,502 "no" votes and 1,093,485 "yes" votes being cast. In 2005, Ohio Democrats, unable to make much headway in regaining seats in the general assembly, decided they would champion an initiative constitutional amendment creating a bipartisan commission to draw legislative district lines. The amendment was crushed at the ballot box by a more than 2-to-1 margin. In 2011, Ohio Democrats and their allies in organized labor, emboldened by their defeat of the Ohio Republicans' efforts to rein in public sector unions, came together again to collect the necessary signatures to place on the ballot an initiative constitutional amendment to create a state-funded commission to draw both state legislative and congressional districts. The amendment was defeated with a "no" vote of 3,088,402 and a "yes" vote of 1,900,105. It is likely that these efforts to reform the redistricting process in Ohio fell short in part because the Ohio voters do not see this as a problem, and the remedy is often complex and confusing. This leads voters to the safe vote of "no."

Term Limits

In November of 1992, three significant and very well supported sets of initiative constitutional amendments were successful on the ballot. These amendments set limits on the number of consecutive terms in office to be served by members of Congress, the state legislature, and all of the statewide elected offices in Ohio. The movement for term limits was sweeping the country, driven by the public's view that office holders were more interested in taking care and protecting their own interests rather than the interests of the public. The first amendment limited the U.S. senator from Ohio to two successive terms in office and a representative to the U.S. house of representatives to four consecutive terms. The second constitutional amendment established identical limits for those in the Ohio senate and house of representatives. An amendment proposed by the general assembly in 1954 already limited the Ohio governor to two successive terms in office. The last of the three initiatives placed on the ballot in 1992 imposed these same limits on the lieutenant governor, secretary of state, attorney general, and auditor. Each of the amendments passed by similar margins, with support from over two-thirds of the voters.

The amendment limiting the terms of U.S. senators and representatives was never implemented. A supreme court decision in 1995 concluded that all such limits on members of Congress ran afoul of the federal Constitution.[7]

Voting Reforms

The rules for the conduct of elections in Ohio have been a source of controversy for decades. A 1914 constitutional amendment by initiative petition in Ohio that proposed to extend suffrage to women received 335,390 "yes" votes and 518,295 "no" votes. In 1915, there was an initiative to limit elections on twice-defeated constitutional proposals and to prevent the abuse of the initiative and referendum. This failed by a "no" vote of 482,275 to 417,384. There was an attempt to have a constitutional amendment by initiative to eliminate the compulsory primary that was also soundly defeated. In 1949, an initiative constitutional amendment was passed by voters eliminating the straight-ticket device, where one vote would cast a ballot for an entire party ticket. Finally, in the 1970s, Ohio adopted Election Day registration. In the 1977 election, the first where that law was in effect, there was a proposed initiative constitutional amendment on the ballot that required a voter to be registered for thirty days prior to an election. That amendment was passed.

Defining and Controlling Illegal and Legal Substances

Although a national constitutional prohibition of alcohol in the United States existed from 1919 to 1933, during most of our history, control of alcohol has been viewed as a reserve power of the states. On the ballot in November of 1914 was a proposed initiative constitutional amendment prohibiting the selling, manufacturing, or importing of intoxicating liquors. That amendment was rejected by a vote of 588,329 to 504,177. Although a similar amendment by initiative was rejected in 1917, a statewide prohibition amendment proposed through the initiative was finally adopted in 1918, one year before national prohibition took hold. The 21st Amendment to the U.S. Constitution was ratified in 1933, ending national prohibition. In that same year, Ohio voters approved an amendment proposed by the general assembly repealing statewide prohibition.[8]

Ohio once allowed the consumption of what was called 3.2 beer (alcohol content had to be at 3.2 percent or below) for eighteen-years-olds. In 1983, an initiative constitutional amendment proposed to raise the minimum age for the consumption of beer in Ohio to twenty-one. That was turned down by voters. Soon after that, the drinking age was raised by the Ohio general assembly because of a threat from the federal government, who said that highway funds would be withheld if the drinking age for all alcohol was not raised to twenty-one.

Ohio's very restrictive limitation on smoking tobacco is the result of the passage of one of the few statutes placed on the ballot by initiative. In 2006, voters supported an initiated state law that restricted smoking in places of employment and most places open to the public.

The illegal substance that might make the ballot in the near future as an initiative constitutional amendment is a proposal to legalize marijuana for medical use. Language for two initiative constitutional amendments has been approved by the Ohio Ballot Board; however, those promoting the issue have not yet gathered enough signatures to place the proposal before Ohio voters.[9] It should be kept in mind that it usually takes a sizable campaign war chest to pay solicitors to collect the necessary signatures to qualify an initiative proposal for the ballot.

Conclusion

Ohioans have voted on numerous constitutional amendments over the past 100 years. Those amendments proposed by the general assembly have had more success than those put forward by initiative. The voters have passed 102 of the 153 amendments advanced by the general assembly. Of the initiative petition constitutional amendments, 53 have been rejected and 19 adopted. The initiative constitutional amendments have not placed the restraints on the legislature that are found in some other states (California, for example) where the initiative is permitted. In 1983, there was an initiative constitutional amendment placed on the ballot to require a three-fifths majority in the general assembly to raise taxes. That proposal was rejected.

It is important to remember that direct democracy in Ohio is not limited to voting on initiatives and referendums. On November 3, 2013, two days before local elections were held in Ohio, columnist Thomas Suddes pointed out that Ohio voters would be confronting 1,677 local issues. These included 308 local liquor options, 1,055 local tax levies, and 65 local income tax questions.[10]

Notes

1. Steven H. Steinglass and Gino Scarselli, *The Ohio State Constitution* (New York: Oxford University Press, 2011), 131.
2. A good source on the history of Ohio constitutional amendments, initiatives, and referendum can be found on the Ohio secretary of state's website (http://www.sos.state.oh.us/) and a document compiled from 1953 through 2014 (http://www.sos.state.oh.us/sos/upload/elections/historical/issuehist.pdf). All of the voting results cited in this chapter were gathered from this document.
3. John H. Fenton, "The Right to Work Vote in Ohio," *Midwest Journal of Political Science* 3, no. 3 (Aug 1959): 241–253.
4. The Ohio Constitution, Article XV, Section 11.
5. "Ohio Casino in Lorain (1990)," Ballotpedia, accessed November 3, 2014, http://www.Ballotpedia.org/Ohio_casino_in_Lorain_(1990)
6. Lucas Sullivan, "Casinos Fall Short of Revenue Projections," *Columbus Dispatch*, December 8, 2013.
7. *U.S. Term Limits Inc. v. Thorton* 514 U.S. 749 (1995).
8. Steinglass and Scarselli, *The Ohio State Constitution*, 60–61.
9. "Group Wants to Decriminalize Marijuana in Toledo," Wn.com, accessed November 7 2014, http://article.wn.com/view/2014/05/10/Group_wants_to_decriminalize_marijuana_in_Toledo_q/
10. Thomas Suddes, "Direct Democracy Hasn't Worked Out as Intended," *Columbus Dispatch*, November 3, 2013.

Index

CQ Press, an imprint of SAGE, is the leading publisher of books, periodicals, and electronic products on American government and international affairs. CQ Press consistently ranks among the top commercial publishers in terms of quality, as evidenced by the numerous awards its products have won over the years. CQ Press owes its existence to Nelson Poynter, former publisher of the *St. Petersburg Times,* and his wife Henrietta, with whom he founded *Congressional Quarterly* in 1945. Poynter established CQ with the mission of promoting democracy through education and in 1975 founded the Modern Media Institute, renamed The Poynter Institute for Media Studies after his death. The Poynter Institute (*www.poynter.org*) is a nonprofit organization dedicated to training journalists and media leaders.

In 2008, CQ Press was acquired by SAGE, a leading international publisher of journals, books, and electronic media for academic, educational, and professional markets. Since 1965, SAGE has helped inform and educate a global community of scholars, practitioners, researchers, and students spanning a wide range of subject areas, including business, humanities, social sciences, and science, technology, and medicine. A privately owned corporation, SAGE has offices in Los Angeles, Boston, London, New Delhi, and Singapore, in addition to the Washington DC office of CQ Press.